16 —

AL-ANON INFORMATION SERVICE
(916) 334-2970

Opening our Hearts

Transforming our Losses

 Al-Anon Family Groups
Hope and help for families and friends of alcoholics

For information and a catalog of literature write to:
Al-Anon Family Group Headquarters, Inc.
1600 Corporate Landing Parkway
Virginia Beach, Virginia 23454-5617
757-563-1600   Fax: 757-563-1655
www.al-anon.alateen.org/members
wso@al-anon.org

Al-Anon/Alateen is supported by members' voluntary contributions and from the sale of our Conference Approved Literature.

Library of Congress Catalog Card No. 2007924183
ISBN-978-0-910034-47-0

Approved by
World Service Conference
Al-Anon Family Groups

Al-Anon books that may be helpful:

Alateen—Hope for Children of Alcoholics (B-3)

The Dilemma of the Alcoholic Marriage (B-4)

The Al-Anon Family Groups—Classic Edition (B-5)

One Day at a Time in Al-Anon (B-6), Large Print (B-14)

Lois Remembers (B-7)

Al-Anon's Twelve Steps & Twelve Traditions (B-8)

Alateen—a day at a time (B-10)

As We Understood . . . (B-11)

. . . In All Our Affairs: Making Crises Work for You (B-15)

Courage to Change—One Day at a Time in Al-Anon II (B-16), Large Print (B-17)

From Survival to Recovery: Growing Up in an Alcoholic Home (B-21)

How Al-Anon Works for Families & Friends of Alcoholics (B-22)

Courage to Be Me—Living with Alcoholism (B-23)

Paths to Recovery—Al-Anon's Steps, Traditions, and Concepts (B-24)

Living Today in Alateen (B-26)

Hope for Today (B-27), Large Print (B-28)

Preamble

The Al-Anon Family Groups are a fellowship of relatives and friends of alcoholics who share their experience, strength, and hope in order to solve their common problems. We believe alcoholism is a family illness and that changed attitudes can aid recovery.

Al-Anon is not allied with any sect, denomination, political entity, organization, or institution; does not engage in any controversy; neither endorses nor opposes any cause. There are no dues for membership. Al-Anon is self-supporting through its own voluntary contributions.

Al-Anon has but one purpose: to help families of alcoholics. We do this by practicing the Twelve Steps, by welcoming and giving comfort to families of alcoholics, and by giving understanding and encouragement to the alcoholic.

Suggested Preamble to the Twelve Steps

Contents

Preface

Alcoholism is a disease of many losses. For those of us who are the relatives and friends of alcoholics, these losses affect many aspects of our lives and remain with us over time, whether or not we are still living with an active alcoholic. In *Opening Our Hearts, Transforming Our Losses*, we share the hope we have found with the help of Al-Anon Family Groups as we came to acknowledge, understand, and accept the losses we experienced.

This book is an exploration of issues that concern everyone who has struggled with someone else's alcoholism. We experience loss from not having had the happy childhood we wanted, from a marriage that fell short of our hopes and dreams, or from the disappointments of other personal relationships that did not meet our expectations.

In coping with these problems, we wondered why unfortunate things were happening to us. We learned to ignore our feelings, create fantasy solutions, and minimize our problems. We assumed that somehow we were at fault—and that no one else could understand our despair. With each loss, we felt more alone and isolated.

This book helps us to acknowledge the painful reality of loss and grief. It encourages us to acknowledge sometimes hidden thoughts and fears, to recognize the truth of our feelings, and to seek solutions that ease our pain and lead us to inner peace.

We experience Al-Anon Family Groups as safe and supportive

places to find shelter along with others who are also on a similar path of self-discovery based on honest searching and sharing. Release from the burden of past trauma is not achieved by denying that those losses occurred. We can move forward to a brighter future by acknowledging the pain of what happened and then leaving it behind. We learn to let go of fantasies of what might have been and to open ourselves to the realities of what is. We find that others have had similar feelings of over-responsibility and guilt. As we come to understand how others have made progress, we gain the inner resources to pull aside the emotional curtain that has kept us separated from the peace of mind that we yearned for and the rich and full life that we deserve.

May this book help you on your journey toward release and hope. As our slogan says, "Together We Can Make It," and as the Suggested Al-Anon/Alateen Closing invites, ". . . Let the understanding, love, and peace of the program grow in you one day at a time."

Introduction

"I finally understood that I needed to give myself permission to grieve."

Grief is a natural response to the many losses that we suffer as a consequence of someone else's alcoholism. Some of us may believe we are to blame for our losses, or that they happen as the result of bad luck. We may find ourselves saying or thinking, "What did I do to deserve this?" Under the cloud of alcoholism, it's easy to lose our dreams of a happy family life and our hopes that the alcoholic will find recovery. We may no longer feel the same intimacy we once felt with our alcoholic partner, child, family member, or friend. Over the long-term, we tend to lose perspective on how alcoholism affects our relationships and our quality of life. The grief that follows in the wake of alcoholism may not seem so obvious a consideration.

Loss as part of the family disease of alcoholism

"Alcoholism robbed me of who I was, caused injury to my daughter, and almost completely destroyed my best friend. It took bits and pieces of us all during those first six years. Those were tremendous losses that took a long time to work through. My grief was immense. I felt inconsolable."

Living with alcoholism on a daily basis affects our sense of dignity and self-respect. Daily we are reminded of how our lives are

3

different than we had hoped or expected. Before long our trust and intimacy begin to erode, and our relationship with the alcoholic starts to deteriorate. Over time the culmination of losses can take its toll on us.

Those of us who grew up in alcoholic homes grieve for our childhoods. Painful memories from our past can consume us with grief, or we may spend years without realizing we are grieving. As children, any change could trigger feelings of loss.

> *"I wanted everything to stay the same and I didn't accept change well. I resented it; talked about how things used to be; and longed for old homes, toys, pets, and fun times."*

Even memories of good times with our families can trigger sadness, since those times were often tainted by the awareness that they wouldn't last. We may feel a sorrow so deep we often can't find the words to speak of it.

It's not just about death

When we first begin to understand how alcoholism has affected our lives, we may not fully recognize our feelings of grief and loss. We may tend to minimize or deny the pain by telling ourselves, "Well, at least she isn't dead," or, "Things could be worse." True, things probably could be worse, but they're also probably tough enough just as they are.

We may understand that we are grieving, or we may be confused by the sudden onset of emotions. One member didn't know why she felt the way she did when her son left home until her Sponsor suggested she might be grieving. Initially startled by this suggestion, she came to realize how her son's years of alcohol abuse had taken him away from her emotionally long before his physical absence. Being able to recognize and name our losses is a vital first step toward facing our grief.

*"Before recovery, I used to think grief only happened when
someone died. I had been in Al-Anon for several years
before I read about grief in relation to alcoholism. It started
to make perfect sense to me when I understood that much of
my sadness, anger, and mixed-up feelings were signs of grief.
I was losing my battle with trying to control the alcoholic
in my life. At last I could see I was grieving. As I got more
and more honest, I saw that I had been in grief much of my
life, but had no name for it. Recognizing my grief seemed
to offer me a sense of dignity. I finally understood what
was happening to me. I now use this knowledge when I
experience small losses or big ones."*

Physical, emotional, and spiritual symptoms of grief

Living with the disease of alcoholism affects us physically, emotionally, and spiritually. Many describe the pain of grief as unlike anything they've ever felt before. Although we may experience similar symptoms, grief will affect each of us differently. Some of us may find it difficult to function, while others are able to continue with routine daily activities.

*"Some days all I could do was sit on the floor and cry
uncontrollably. Yet funeral arrangements had to be made,
and I needed to tend to daily life. Bills had to be paid and
laundry had to be done. I had to eat. I conducted all my
activities through a veil of grief. During that time, I learned
that doing the next right thing was enough. I also learned
that support was only a phone call or a meeting away. Some
days the only thing I was capable of doing was meeting an
Al-Anon member for a cup of coffee. I learned to be gentle
with myself. On any given day, working my program to the
best of my ability is all I can do."*

One overwhelming fear for many of us is that we'll always feel this way and that we will never recover. Or we may, for a time, not *want* to feel better. One member felt this way after her husband's death: "It had been a willful refusal on my part to allow myself to be consoled. I met every attempt with the words, 'Yes, but.' Though it may be true that others could be consoled, I believed my loss was so much greater than theirs. My grief had turned into the 'Poor Me's,' which kept me from taking action to help myself feel better."

Grief is exhausting. It can make us sleepless or make it difficult to get out of bed. We may forget to eat, or we may overeat. We may not feel like taking a shower, going to work, or preparing a meal. Grief is unpredictable. We may feel sad one minute, then angry or confused the next. When we have a moment alone, we may find that we can't stop crying. One day we may wake up feeling some relief, and the next find ourselves depressed.

"I would find myself crying any time I became relaxed—as in not busy. I couldn't just sit and rest because I would start crying. I would even cry while I was driving. I would get angry with myself for grieving, telling myself I shouldn't feel that way!"

Fear, confusion, and lack of concentration can accompany us for months. We may become forgetful and irritable. One member couldn't remember how to perform the simplest tasks, like turning on an electronic appliance. Depression and anxiety are also common. We may lose interest in activities we once found enjoyable and may need to isolate for a while. We may need to spend some days in our pajamas. At times like these, family and work demands can feel particularly burdensome. If we can't take care of ourselves, how can we possibly take care of anyone or anything else? Some days we may question how we'll get through the day. If our depression continues to worsen, if life seems too much to bear, or if we feel like giving up, we may need to seek professional help.

A spiritual perspective can be a source of strength and support for many of us while we are grieving. Although some of us feel more connected to our Higher Power at this time, others may become angry or may even question our Higher Power's presence in our lives. If we are feeling disconnected spiritually, this situation is not cause for alarm or shame. Whatever we are feeling is okay and transitory. As our program reminds us, "This too shall pass."

Grief and loss in the journey toward recovery

When we first entered the rooms of Al-Anon, our attempts at managing our lives on our own were no longer working. By reaching out for help, we took the first step toward our healing. We soon learned that our recovery depends upon our readiness to focus on ourselves. If we're uncomfortable with our feelings, we may try to find ways to distract ourselves from them.

"When I stopped running, I finally had to feel my feelings. I talked to my Sponsor a lot, and trusted that my Higher Power would get me through this rough time."

As newcomers to Al-Anon, we may experience so many feelings at once that it may take some time to sort through them. Similarly, those of us who have been recovering for a while may have moments when we question whether our program is working for us. Although this can feel scary, it doesn't mean our recovery is at stake. If we've been unaware of our losses until now, we may have years of unexpressed feelings to face. We don't have to confront everything at once. We are not in a race to the finish line. With our Higher Power's guidance, we can work our program at our own pace, in our own way. We can be patient and gentle with ourselves, trusting that wherever we are is exactly where we are supposed to be.

In Al-Anon we come to recognize that grief is a natural part of life, not a punishment. If we look around us, we'll see that all living creatures experience loss. A robin's egg falls from its nest before it is hatched; a mother deer is hit by a car, leaving her young fawn to fend for itself.

We are not exempt from suffering. Whatever loss we may be grieving, with Al-Anon we don't have to face it alone. We can take comfort in knowing that our grief means we're truly dealing with our loss and not denying it. When our lives feel disrupted and chaotic, the clear and simple principles of our program can ground us. Much like a compass, our slogans, Steps, Traditions, and Concepts of Service can help us navigate through the turbulent waters of grief and loss.

As we learn from experience, it is our grief that connects us to each other. It doesn't have to isolate us. When we share our pain with other people, we are truly heard and understood—perhaps for the first time. As we learn to apply the Al-Anon tools, we discover that no situation is truly hopeless. In fact, many of us have been able to find hope in the midst of despair and serenity in the face of grief.

How to use this book

Like all our Al-Anon Conference Approved Literature, this book represents the collective wisdom of our members. The stories shared here reflect the experience, strength, and hope of hundreds of us. How we choose to incorporate this book into our lives is entirely up to us. Some of us may read it from cover to cover. Others may want to read a chapter that speaks more directly to a specific aspect of their grief. If we are in the depths of grief right now, one page, one paragraph, or a sentence at a time may be all that we can handle. Whatever our present circumstance, respect for where we are and what we need in the moment is of the utmost importance.

All quotes throughout the book are from Al-Anon members, unless otherwise noted. Members' stories are presented at the conclusion of each chapter, followed by a list of questions intended as suggestions for meditation and reflection. Rather than trying to tackle every question at once, we might choose to begin or end our day by taking time to reflect on one or two that are most relevant to us. We can always return to the other questions at a later time. We may also wish to use these questions as topics for discussion at meetings or with our Sponsor. Turning to the index can be useful if we're struggling with a particular feeling, or if we're seeking insight into the Steps, slogans, or other Al-Anon tools.

Whatever we might be going through right now, we can rest assured that there are those among us who have felt what we are feeling. As the Suggested Al-Anon/Alateen Closing for meetings states, if we keep an open mind, we can find help. We will find "that there is no situation too difficult to be bettered and no unhappiness too great to be lessened." We may struggle at times with believing this to be true, but we can find hope from those who have walked this path before us. As we begin to heal from our losses, we in turn offer this same hope to others. Through our willingness to face our loss openly and honestly, we discover our strength and resilience—not *despite* it, but *because* of it.

Grief as a Process

*"My journey through grief is much like my
journey through recovery."*

We may or may not be aware of our losses when we step into our first Al-Anon meeting. It may take several weeks or many years in the program before they surface. Some of us were taught that it's not okay to cry or to be angry. As a result, we may have become adept at showing the world a smiling face while masking our true emotions. Grief has its own timing. We can trust that we'll become aware of our losses when we're ready to deal with them.

> *"Before Al-Anon, I was stuck. When my mom died, I pretended to move on, but I felt like a three-year-old in an adult's body. I felt inconsolable, scared, lost, and inadequate."*

In Al-Anon, we hear a lot about dealing with our feelings, but getting comfortable with our feelings can take time. The mere thought of having to feel our suppressed emotions might seem frightening at first. It may initially feel easier and more comfortable to let our lives continue as they are, even if we know deep down that this is not in our best interest. However, our anxiety can be lessened as we witness other members sharing their feelings openly. Over time the validation and acceptance we receive in Al-Anon can help us feel more comfortable with sharing our own thoughts and feelings.

It can be helpful to look at our grief in the same way as our recovery. If it took time to get where we are today, we can't expect to get better overnight. "Progress Not Perfection" reminds us that our recovery is not an event, but a process. All that's required of us is to do the best we can today, even if that means just getting ourselves to a meeting or reading a page from our literature. Sometimes the smallest steps are the ones that can bring us the most comfort.

Admitting our grief

> *"Before Al-Anon, I couldn't face my own grief or loss. Instead, I quickly and totally denied it. To admit my losses would*

have felt like I was 'less than.' I believed there was one 'right'
way to handle these feelings and I didn't know what that
way was."

Though there is no single way to approach our grief, the
Al-Anon tools can help us find our way. Step One helps us come
to understand that we are powerless over our losses, just as we are
powerless over alcoholism. Trying to control our grief has only
made our lives unmanageable. We spent years being the responsible ones, trying to hold things together for our families, so we may
find it difficult to give up our control. If we've been accustomed
to handling everything on our own, we may find it difficult at first
to ask for help. Yet the more we try to control our grief, the more
we seem to suffer. Admitting that we are grieving is admitting we
are *not* in control. Once we realize this, we can begin to feel some
relief from the burden of carrying everything on our shoulders.

The recurring nature of grief

"I am invited to grieve with every change in life. Often I ignore
the invitation, deciding the particular change is 'no big
deal,' or telling myself, 'I can handle this.' Sometimes the
culmination of all the 'little' changes I haven't addressed
hits me all at once. I find myself overreacting to a person or
situation, becoming depressed or just irritable."

It is often these "little" changes that catch us by surprise. They
seem to come out of nowhere. The day-in and day-out disappointments and broken promises of living with an alcoholic can
become commonplace, until one day we wake up feeling the
effect of all those "small" losses. Why, we wonder, do we suddenly
feel sad about our situation, especially when we may have spent
months or even years living this way?

Many of us have lived with the notion that grief is something
we feel when we have lost something tangible—when someone

has died or gone away. In Al-Anon we learn that although the alcoholic may still be living, he or she is unable to be fully present—emotionally, spiritually, or even physically. Recognizing that we are not living the lives we had planned or hoped for with the person we love is a loss that occurs gradually. Each day we lose a little bit more until what remains is merely a shadow of the person or life we thought we knew. Living with ongoing grief of this kind can be particularly trying.

"One Day at a Time" can help us through these difficult days. We get ahead of ourselves when we worry about how we will get through tomorrow or next week. We can't know what tomorrow will bring. What a relief it is to know we only have to deal with today. Though getting through today might feel like getting through all of eternity, we can remind ourselves that we won't feel this way forever. We can trust that our Higher Power has a plan for us, even if we can't see where we are headed.

When an old loss revisits us

Our grief from past losses can come upon us unexpectedly— sometimes after many years. If we faced a loss in the past, we may be wondering why we are still in pain. We may have thought we had worked through our grief, and here it is again. Without realizing it, we may start reacting in old, familiar ways. Our former habits and fears return—the same response we had when reacting to alcoholism. We may become overly focused on others to the point of neglecting ourselves, and our attempt to control can quickly take over. Our obsessive worrying may return, and we find our time and energy going toward anticipating tomorrow's troubles.

Often, acceptance of our losses arrives in stages. Such realizations would likely overwhelm us if they were to occur all at once, just as trying to grasp the entirety of the program all at once would be too much for most of us. In this way, the cyclical or recurring nature of grief may be our Higher Power's way of protecting us from having to face too much all at once. Just because an old loss has resurfaced doesn't mean we are back where we started. It simply means we're being asked to face another aspect of our grief that we may not have been ready to face until now.

Questioning our recovery

After we've been recovering for a while, there may come a time when we question whether the program is still working for us. We may find ourselves wondering why we don't feel happier. After all, we tried so hard to accept our situation, worked the Steps, and attended meetings. We wonder if sadness is all there is to show for our efforts.

Such feelings may be frightening and alarming. Our first impulse may be to dismiss them. However, many of us have discovered the importance of honoring what our feelings are trying to tell us. Questioning can actually be an important turning point in our recovery. It can teach us about where we are headed, can signal us to slow down, or can prompt us to take better care of ourselves. Just as a marathon swimmer needs to float in order to rest and regain strength, so too will we need to find moments to renew ourselves. We may need to take mental and emotional breaks here and there to allow ourselves to regroup or refocus our energies.

Experience has taught many of us that recovery is not a straight and narrow path. Undoubtedly, we will be asked to make unexpected, but necessary, turns along the way. As we strive to turn our will and our lives over to the care of a Higher Power, we will be given many opportunities to practice doing so. We may not always know where we are headed in our recovery or grief, but we can learn to trust that we are being led to a better place than where we started.

Giving ourselves time to grieve

The time each of us needs to grieve will vary from person to person. We may have been told that it takes a year to grieve the death of a loved one, only to find ourselves still in pain three years later. We don't need to set deadlines for our grief, and we don't have to accept anyone else's timelines. While one person may be able to apply the Steps and find serenity in a matter of hours or minutes, for another, it may take months or even years. Chances are we will have to re-apply the wisdom of the Steps and slogans to our particular situation not just once, but again and again. Just as each of us makes progress in Al-Anon in our own way and pace, so too will each of us approach grief differently.

One member kept her husband's belongings in her garage for over a year after his death. Letting go of her urgency and allowing the belongings to stay in her garage were crucial to her grieving process. Her understanding of the program allowed her to keep his things for as long as she needed. After some time passed, she was able to make decisions about what to keep and what to donate. We do ourselves a great disservice when we compare our grief to anyone else's. While we gain hope from others, it helps to keep in mind that no two losses are alike and that no one has experienced our loss. We can trust that whatever time it takes for us to grieve will be exactly what we need.

> *"Gradually, I took Al-Anon's suggestions to get in touch with my feelings, and for a while I felt worse than ever. As I started to see what I was gaining instead of just what I was losing, I didn't feel quite so bad. But it was a slow process made slower by my reluctance to follow the suggestions of fellow members."*

There may be times when giving ourselves over entirely to our feelings might prevent us from being able to function in our daily lives. At such times, one member decided to allow herself 15 minutes to be totally and completely immersed in her grief. After those

15 minutes, she would let it go and move on to something else. If she struggled to let go, she would allow herself another 15 minutes and would try again. This exercise allowed her to express whatever she was feeling without allowing her feelings to control her.

In Al-Anon we learn not to deny our feelings. We can be honest with ourselves and others about where we are in our grief. We don't have to pretend that everything is fine or that we're handling everything perfectly. When asked about how she was doing after her husband died, one member responded, "Not good. But I'm just trying to do what I need to do until I feel like doing it." While some of our friends, family, or coworkers may question why we are still grieving, in Al-Anon we are not judged or rushed through our grief.

> *"What a relief to be able to cry and not have to worry that people were thinking I should be 'over that' by now. My Al-Anon friends listened to me and accepted me right where I was."*

Members share experience, strength, and hope: Grief as a process

When I think of grief, I think of awareness, acceptance, and action. Sometimes when I feel annoyed, irritated, or angry, these feelings are a mask for my grief. I often deny my grief because it is too painful. I try to remember that acting out by yelling at my child or blaming my spouse is more painful in the long run than feeling the grief. I try to pause when I get annoyed and ask myself what's really going on within me.

My Sponsor says that what we resist persists. When I choose to push away my feelings of grief, they keep coming back in various forms. Acceptance helps. Treating myself like a best friend or small child who is grieving gives me permission to accept that I am hurting. When I ask for help, I am taking action in my own best interest. I surrender to my feelings, give myself a big inward hug, and let myself cry. I pray to my Higher Power or call an Al-Anon friend. If I am not ready to surrender, I pray for willingness. My Higher Power gives me the time and space to grieve when I am ready.

For years I felt like I was carrying around a huge weight. My life was totally out of control. Finally, I realized that I needed to feel the feelings of grief and loss I had been running from. I had to stop trying to mask and dull my emotional pain. I knew I had years of feelings to catch up on. My search to make sense of what I was experiencing led me to the rooms of Al-Anon. There I discovered that the true source of my intense pain was not so much the losses I had suffered, but rather the ways I had attempted to cope with them by trying to control other people and events.

What's helped me heal are feeling my feelings, reading on the subject of loss, sharing at meetings and with close friends, taking gentle care of myself, and journaling. Al-Anon's slogans have been central to my healing. I repeat them whenever my feelings seem overwhelming or a situation seems too much to bear. I still carry the memories of my losses, but I have healed so much. I've learned not to let the fear of loss take control of my life anymore. I keep turning it all over to God and working the program, and my life continues to get better.

Questions for reflection and meditation
- What am I grieving today?
- Have I admitted my powerlessness over my grief, or am I trying to control it?
- Am I giving myself time to grieve without worrying about how long it "should" take?
- When was the last time I shared my grief with a trusted loved one, my Sponsor, my Higher Power, or at an Al-Anon meeting?
- What can I do today to be gentle with myself?

Living with the Family Disease of Alcoholism

"When I first dragged myself into the rooms of Al-Anon, I discovered that alcoholics had three choices: institutions, death, or recovery. I had the same three options. I chose recovery. I didn't like the alternatives."

Living with alcoholism can feel like we're in a constant state of mourning. We may have become so adept at living with loss that we go about our days unaware of its presence. When we admit that our lives are affected by someone else's drinking, we are also admitting our grief. Because alcoholism is a family disease, all members of the family are affected, not just the alcoholic. Each person reacts in his or her own way in response to the alcoholic environment. One may try to control, while another may deny there's even a problem. Others will blame themselves.

Before Al-Anon, we kept ourselves busy seeking solutions for the alcoholic. When what we were trying to accomplish wasn't succeeding, we told ourselves to work harder or to try something else. We may even have told ourselves it was our fault if we couldn't convince the alcoholic to get sober. If we could only find the right words at the right time, relayed in just the right tone of voice, then maybe we could get the alcoholic to see things our way. Desperate to fulfill our dreams for a happy family life, we thought that devoting all our energy to the problem was the answer. Little did we know we were actually contributing to the problem by trying to force solutions.

In Al-Anon we learn that we didn't cause the alcoholism in our lives, we can't control it, and we can't cure it. If we're trying to force solutions, we can remember "Easy Does It." Though we can't expect our lives to always be easy, this slogan suggests that everything doesn't have to be so hard all the time either. "Easy Does It" reminds us to be gentle with ourselves. We don't have to try harder or do better. We have tried long and hard enough. Though we may not be able to change the alcoholic, we discover there is one person we can change—ourselves.

A disease of losses

"My first husband died an alcoholic, but I didn't grieve his death so much as I grieved our failed relationship and my dreams of love, happiness, and 'til death do us part' that

hadn't come true. I grieved with anger, resentment, and the 'why me's' for years, not understanding that the disease of alcoholism had been the real problem. This disease ended our relationship and my husband's life."

The effects of alcoholism permeate our relationships and can complicate our grief. We mourn for ourselves, for our dreams, and for our families. If we have young children, they may already be experiencing the consequences of growing up in an alcoholic home. Even if our children are no longer living with active alcoholism, their lives continue to be affected. They may withdraw, blame themselves, struggle at school, or act out in negative ways. Our grown children may also be carrying the painful burden of the family disease into their adult lives. The very qualities that once helped them survive can later cause problems in relationships with family, friends, and coworkers. They might have trouble making decisions. They might struggle with fear and anxiety, or have difficulty maintaining intimate relationships. They often marry alcoholics or become alcoholics themselves.

Living day-to-day with alcoholism damages our self-esteem. By the time we come to Al-Anon, we may feel like we have lost ourselves. It is admirable to be considerate and attentive to the needs of others, but not at the expense of our own well-being. Little by little, we may have neglected our own needs and instead gave all our love, care, and attention to others. We may not be entirely sure how we got to this point.

"I recognized I had not only lost what control I thought I had, but I had lost myself. The very addiction I wanted to end was being fueled by my behavior. Al-Anon has helped me see the part I played in the nightmare I had been living in and gave me the tools to help me wake up and start living life on life's terms, not mine. Today, I can look in the mirror and know I am reclaiming what once had been lost—myself."

Changing the dynamics of our relationships

In Al-Anon we learn how to set boundaries, to say yes when we mean yes, and no when we mean no. We no longer give to others out of obligation, control, or fear, but because we want to give. Once we begin to take better care of ourselves, we can begin to give to others in healthier ways.

Recognizing our part in the alcoholic relationship is a crucial component of our recovery. Before we can make positive changes, we must first become aware of the dynamics of the relationship and the role we've been playing. Perhaps we were enablers who rescued or made excuses for the alcoholic. Or we may have seen ourselves as victims, helpless to change our circumstances. Maybe our role was to accept all the blame for the alcoholic's drinking or bad behavior, apologizing for anything that went wrong. Some of our conduct made a bad situation worse.

We examine our role in the family disease not to blame ourselves, but rather to deepen our understanding and compassion for those parts of ourselves we want to change. We cannot break our old patterns without such understanding. Rather than continuing to feel responsible for others, we begin to take responsibility for ourselves and our own actions. We did the best we could at the time with the resources we had, but now that we are aware, we can see another way. As we apply the principles of our program to our day-to-day lives, we begin to respond to situations differently than we had in the past. We give up our illusions of control and our belief that we can change the alcoholic or force sobriety.

As we begin to change, so too will our relationships—not just with the alcoholic, but with everyone around us. In any relationship, when one person changes, the entire relationship is altered. Just as we have been affected by the family disease of alcoholism, those around us will be affected by our recovery as we begin to heal. Even though we may want a change in our relationship, the change itself can be a loss.

Not everyone will be happy about the new changes in us—including ourselves at times. We may reminisce about how things used to be and may even try to convince ourselves that things weren't so bad before recovery. We can expect a temporary period of upset or increased crisis at this time. This doesn't mean we should go back to the way things were, though we may be feeling pressure to do so. Positive changes don't always feel right at first. On those days when going back may seem easier, we can trust that our Higher Power has guided us to this point in our lives. We are precisely where we need to be.

Coping with uncertainty and crisis

When living with active alcoholism, life can sometimes feel like nothing more than one crisis after another. In fact, we can become so accustomed to living in crisis mode that we feel uneasy if we're not in the midst of chaos. When faced with a crisis or traumatic event, many of us became skilled at putting our feelings on hold. Often what we felt came second to managing the crisis. Gradually we may have lost touch with our ability to honor our feelings. Our first impulse may be to react immediately instead of pausing to consider our options. We might tend to perceive minor incidents as major catastrophes.

As we gain more insight, we learn at Al-Anon meetings how to respond differently than we did in the past. We can take a moment to consider our feelings, even in the midst of a crisis. Our slogan "Think" reminds us there are few situations that demand an immediate response from us. We can give ourselves some time—even if it's only a few minutes—to consider how we would like to handle the situation. Rather than simply reacting out of old habits, we find that by examining our feelings, we can better handle any crisis that comes our way. When we stop to "Think" before we act, we are more likely to make decisions that are in our own best interest.

If things at home seem to be falling apart, we can at least attend a meeting where we can be in a place of peace, surrounded by the loving support and comfort of other members. The simple act of going to a meeting can be an act of caring, and the benefits of taking time for ourselves can go a long way.

"Day-by-day, week-by-week, I'm finding bits and pieces of serenity that had been so elusive for so many years. With time, I trust that those pieces will grow as I put the Al-Anon principles to work in my life. I've seen and learned enough to believe that this program will take me where I'm meant to go, free me from my misery, and restore my love for life."

After admitting our powerlessness in Step One, we are becoming ready to let a Higher Power intervene on our behalf. In taking Step Two, we come to believe a Power greater than ourselves can restore our sanity. These Steps offer hope even in the midst of despair.

Whatever our definition of a Higher Power may be, the one thing most of us have in common is our desire for a more serene life. This can mean different things for each of us. For some, it might mean stepping out of our customary roles and learning how to respond differently to our alcoholic families. For others, it could mean making a commitment to take better care of ourselves and to cultivate healthier relationships with people who love and accept us for who we are.

When faced with the next crisis, we may feel uncertain about our decision to respond differently. If we focus on taking care of ourselves, who will take care of everyone else? We can remind ourselves that in practicing any new behavior, we may feel tentative at first; but the more we practice, the easier it becomes. Eventually we realize that we weren't really in control of anyone else to begin with.

Moving out of chaos

Some of us are so accustomed to living with chaos, it's difficult to imagine our lives without it. Just as the alcoholic has become dependent upon alcohol, we can become dependent upon the chaos. Up until now, we may not have had much experience with serenity. Even when things are going well, we may unconsciously look for ways to sabotage ourselves by creating a crisis. If we feel even remotely peaceful, we may fear it is the calm before the storm. We wait in anxious anticipation that something is about to go wrong. Though this may not feel good, it feels familiar and comfortable. The last thing we want is to be caught off guard and unprepared. Our constant focus on crisis situations—whether real, anticipated, or self-created—ultimately keeps us from focusing on ourselves.

The only way some of us got any attention from our families or friends was when we were in the midst of a crisis. This may have reinforced our belief that we were only worthy of comfort when we were emotional wrecks. It may have taken these repeated encounters with crisis and chaos to get us into the rooms of Al‑Anon. Many of us arrive feeling mentally, emotionally, physically, and spiritually exhausted. Al‑Anon may feel like a last resort. But it is here we learn that we don't have to wait until we are completely worn‑out or fed‑up to give ourselves the attention we deserve.

If we feel shame over the chaos in our lives, we may find it difficult to share what we're going through with others, particularly those closest to us. Not everyone in our lives will be familiar with the effects of alcoholism. Those around us may wonder why we don't do something more drastic to change our circumstances. In Al‑Anon we are relieved to find that others can hear our pain without giving advice.

Our relationship with a Sponsor can also be extremely helpful as we learn to focus on ourselves. Our Sponsor is someone who has made a commitment to walk beside us on our recovery journey, someone who can help us as we learn to apply the principles of the program to our lives. This one-on-one relationship built on mutual respect allows us to share our personal stories and struggles in more detail.

Prayer and meditation have saved many of us from the obsession and worry that so often accompany a crisis. When we are in the middle of chaos, it can be difficult to stop and take time out to meditate. One simple prayer that has helped so many of us is the Serenity Prayer. It's easy to memorize, and repeating it can have a calming effect, especially if we're in the midst of a crisis:

God, grant me the serenity
To accept the things I cannot change,
Courage to change the things I can,
And wisdom to know the difference.

In this simple prayer, the first thing we ask of our Higher Power is the gift of serenity. We ask not for our situation to change, but rather for the power to change how *we* respond to the situation. This request indicates our desire for peace of mind, for our Higher Power to show us another way to respond. In taking the time to recite this prayer, we are allowing our minds to focus on something else, even if just for a moment. It is possible to find serenity, even in the midst of chaos. We don't have to live in a state of constant vigilance. With the help of Al-Anon, today we have a choice.

Living with chronic illness due to alcoholism

Alcoholism is a three-fold disease: physical, emotional, and spiritual. Long-term alcohol abuse can take its toll on the alcoholic and can lead to chronic illness. But chronic illness due to prolonged drinking does not just affect the active alcoholic. Those who have been sober for years can also be affected. Even before our loved one's illness became a reality, many of us dreaded the day we might receive such news. A medical crisis could serve as a wake-up call for the alcoholic and can often be the motivation to seek recovery. For others, healthcare professionals have repeatedly warned our loved one of potential health problems, only to have those warnings ignored or denied.

It pains us to see our loved one continue drinking, despite those warnings of impending sickness or even death. Daily we fear for the health of our loved one, and we may feel as if we are witnessing a slow suicide. We find it difficult not to project what might go wrong tomorrow, or what will be required of us if our loved one becomes physically ill. Some of us may have promised ourselves we would leave if the drinking were to become unbearable. But if our loved one becomes sick, we may not want to leave or feel that we can.

Some of us have no support network until we come to Al-Anon. Constantly tending to the alcoholic may have left us with little time to nurture relationships with family or friends. When dealing with the onset of an illness, we may feel we have nowhere to turn. Al-Anon can give us the support and encouragement that's been missing from our lives.

> *"I felt at home in Al-Anon from the start. Having a supportive place for me was a new experience. It was like a warm, comforting blanket enveloping me. I was surprised to find that the other members were just like me."*

With so much of our attention going to the alcoholic, we may have left little or none for ourselves. The continual monitoring of others can make us sick. Unintentionally, we may start neglecting our basic needs, such as eating properly, exercising, spending time alone, or engaging in activities we enjoy. In Al-Anon we learn that we are worthy of the same quality of care we offer others.

If we are caring for a loved one who is chronically ill, we may need to remind ourselves daily to take care of ourselves too. Getting to extra meetings, taking an evening for ourselves, or meeting our Sponsor or an Al-Anon friend for coffee are just a few ways we can get some nurturing and support. When we can't get to a meeting or talk with our Sponsor, we can turn to our literature, which is always available to us. We may be surprised to find that reading just one or two pages can help us feel less alone. Though chronic illness may continue to be a daily companion in our lives, we can remind ourselves that so too is the Al-Anon program.

Anticipatory grief

Anticipating the next thing that could go wrong is all too common for those of us who live or have lived with alcoholism. We fear getting a phone call in the middle of the night telling us our loved one has been in a car accident. Or we worry whether the alcoholic will fly into a violent rage upon returning home. All sorts of tragic scenarios may run through our heads on any given day. We may fear that the drinking will continue, resulting in misery and heartache for us.

Living with the fear of what might happen can be emotional static. It occupies our minds and blocks us from moving forward. We may be watching our loved one die a slow death before our eyes. Even if our loved one finds sobriety, we may be surprised to find out that our anxiety and fear have not left us. Unresolved resentments and new fears that the alcoholic will relapse can quickly take the place of our previous worries.

"Keep It Simple" reminds us to look at what is actually happening, rather than what might happen. Sometimes a genuine crisis will demand our attention and force us to act immediately. More often than not, we can let go of our sense of urgency. We can take a breath or two, ask our Higher Power for guidance, and decide calmly what step to take next.

Fear is an instinct that often alerts us to danger. In Al-Anon we learn how to practice living in the moment and letting go of our fears about the future. Before we can do this, we must acknowledge how our former way of life has affected us. For many of us, anticipating what could go wrong may have helped us survive. Staying alert to our environment and the mood of the alcoholic may have protected us from dangerous situations.

Constantly anticipating the next violent episode makes it difficult to find time to reflect on our choices. Some of us have found that time apart from the alcoholic helped us discern what steps to take in order to turn our lives around for the better. If we are living with violence, we may need to seek professional help or make immediate choices to ensure our welfare and the safety of our children. We do not have to tolerate abusive behavior. If necessary, we can leave. Whatever we decide, Al-Anon will be there to support us. Many of us have found that as we apply the Al-Anon principles, solutions come to us that we couldn't have seen on our own—no matter how much thinking we did.

Once we become aware of our propensity toward fear and worry, we can begin to take steps to change our attitudes. In Step Four, we make a "searching and fearless moral inventory of ourselves." By applying this Step to our fear and worry, we gain insights that might otherwise go unexamined. In this Step, we can reflect on what might be preventing us from letting go of our anxiety. We can thank our fears for protecting us and ask our Higher Power to remove them.

As many of us can attest, giving ourselves over to stress, anxiety, and worry doesn't make our lives any easier. "One Day at a Time" reminds us that we can handle most situations for a 24-hour period. Putting this slogan into practice can be especially helpful as we strive to manage our fear and worry. If we think about any endeavor in terms of forever, it will seem insurmountable—but "Just for Today" we can handle almost anything.

The quality of our recovery depends so much upon our changed attitudes. The alcoholics in our lives may or may not get sober.

They may continue to drink despite their failing health, and despite our trying to convince them to change. But we don't have to give up on ourselves. Al-Anon reminds us that we do have choices, even when it seems like we don't. Though we may not be able to abolish our fears altogether, we don't have to let them control us. We no longer have to submit to a life full of fear, apprehension, and anxiety.

The gift of detachment

In Al-Anon we hear a lot about detaching with love. Nevertheless, we may find this particularly difficult to do while we are suffering a sense of loss. We may have been so accustomed to exerting our will and energy trying to make things better, it may now seem like we're being asked to do nothing or to stop caring. It can help to remember that when we detach, we are putting in our Higher Power's care that person, place, or thing we cannot control and never had control of in the first place.

Detaching may simply mean taking a moment to decide how we want to respond, rather than immediately reacting. It may mean not taking everything the alcoholic says or does personally. Detaching with love means that we can hate the disease of alcoholism, yet still feel compassion for the alcoholic. We can let them know we love them, even though we don't love the actions they are taking.

"Let Go and Let God" can help us as we begin to practice loving detachment. Admitting we are powerless doesn't mean we are helpless. We can still take positive action by praying for the alcoholic and ourselves, by respecting ourselves and setting limits. Detaching with love doesn't mean we stop loving the alcoholic, nor does it imply passivity on our part. On the contrary, detachment is a powerful act of love—for us and the alcoholic.

*"I placed my husband in God's hands where he has a much
better chance at a sober life."*

Members share experience, strength, and hope: Living with the family disease of alcoholism

I walked into my first Al-Anon meeting because I was in so much fear that my spouse would die from the disease of alcoholism. I wasn't able to sleep at night because this was all I could think and dream about. My grief would come at any moment of the day, and I would suddenly find myself crying. This worried me because I had always been a happy and positive person. Because of the disease, I started to become mean and isolated. I didn't want to have friends and didn't want to talk to anyone.

Al-Anon changed my life. When I shared my fears of the alcoholic's death, people listened. Soon I found that I didn't have anything more to say about my fears. I started listening to others. People seemed to be happy. There was laughter at meetings. So I kept coming back. I began to work the program and to ask my Higher Power for help. Eventually my anger and fear of losing my spouse lifted. My favorite slogan is "Let Go and Let God." This helps me keep the focus on myself and helps me mind my own business. As for my feelings of loss, I know now that I can feel these feelings, but I can also go on living.

I came to Al-Anon to try and stop my mom from drinking herself to death. As her firstborn child and only son, I felt a strong sense of responsibility for her. By the grace of my Higher Power and the help I received from the program, by the time she did die, I had been in Al-Anon for 20 years. Neither of us were the same as when I first joined.

The last years of my mom's life were sober, but not without health problems. Many of them were probably caused or worsened by her drinking years. I became her primary caregiver. Fortunately by then, I had learned the difference between caregiving and caretaking. Nonetheless, there were times when I struggled with my role. Why was I the one who was relied on most of the time? Why weren't my siblings doing more of their fair share? Shouldn't I be taking care of myself instead of once again looking after my mom, as I had as a child during the drinking?

Ultimately the answer I arrived at was that it was my *choice* to care for her. It didn't matter if anyone else was doing it, because when I really thought about it, I knew I wanted to be there with her. Giving care to her—through the convalescent home stays, the hospital visits, and the first days back home recuperating—was also a way of giving to myself. I knew that eventually there would come a day when I would give anything in the world to have even one more minute with her, and that it would no longer be possible.

Giving myself that time with my mother was a special gift that I now look back on with gratitude and love. Thanks to Al-Anon, I could pay attention to my despair and frustration as the daily caregiving wore on me and take little breaks when possible. But I could also enjoy each moment—"One Day at a Time"—that I still had with her. As a result, I have had no regrets, knowing that in my actions I was being true to myself as well as to my mom.

When my husband went into a treatment program, I experienced living alone for the first time in 27 years. Everything seemed so much harder—walking the dog alone, paying the bills, mowing the lawn. I'd always considered myself a competent woman, but these ordinary jobs made me feel incompetent and insecure. I feared that if I didn't return from my walk, no one would miss me. When I paid the bills, I felt overwhelmed by how much money we spent each month. One day, after numerous failed attempts to start the lawn mower, I stood in the garage fighting back tears of frustration. It was then I knew I needed to ask for help.

When my husband returned home, he was a different man—very fragile and anxious—and I realized that our relationship would have to change. I worried about burdening him even more with my issues. He then told me that at the treatment center he had replaced drinking with smoking. I was shocked and terrified. He had quit smoking 15 years earlier when his doctor told him he wouldn't live to see 50 if he didn't. I felt overwhelmed again by his decision.

In Al-Anon I've learned to stay in the day. Every day I remind myself to be grateful for the good life I have. I do have a sober husband who loves me, and I do have today, which is as good as I choose to make it. If I dwell in those dark places of fear and apprehension, I miss out on opportunities for joy.

My grief and loss started three years before my husband's death, when he became a full-blown alcoholic. I felt the loss of doing fun things together, and for the way our lives used to be. Being blamed for everything—especially "driving him to drink"—turned into madness on my part. What could I do to stop this? My oldest son dragged me to Al-Anon, and what an awakening I had. I learned that I didn't cause my husband's alcoholism. He was a very sick man whom I could neither help nor cure. With Al-Anon's help, I became somewhat happy again. I found that I wasn't alone in this sad situation. My husband died of a massive heart attack while I was walking our dog. It was hard on me, but with Al-Anon, I got through it. Now, I can even remember our happy times together, and I know my husband is in a better place.

By the time I came to Al-Anon, I had lost most of what was near and dear to my heart. My wife's drinking had gotten worse. She had been in and out of rehab and only continued to relapse. I saw no way out of the situation. I was unable to see my part in all this chaos and didn't think I needed any help with what I felt was her problem. I couldn't see how sick I had become—so filled with anxiety and resentment. When my wife agreed to attend an out-of-town rehab, I thought my troubles would be over.

After she left, I felt a tremendous sense of loss. I wasn't sure if she was ever coming back, and I had no one to take care of anymore. I had spent so many years focused on saving her that I had lost who I was. Soon after, my mother took her own life. She had also struggled with alcoholism, and it became too much for her. The loss was more than I could have imagined. I was out of answers.

Then I remembered that my wife had suggested Al-Anon to me on several occasions. I finally surrendered and went to my first meeting—apprehensive, but willing to listen. What a surprise! People were laughing and smiling, some with even worse problems than mine. I made a commitment to try six meetings, and I've been going ever since. As I began to read the literature and talk to other members, I started to see that I was not responsible for my wife's drinking. She had her own Higher Power and her own path to follow.

What kept me sane and coming back that first year was "Progress Not Perfection." I used to feel I always had to be perfect, but in Al-Anon no one expected perfection from me. Today I turn to my Higher Power, recognizing that I'm no longer in charge. I have a Sponsor and work the Steps to the best of my ability. My life has gotten better and my wife came back. We have recovery in our home today. I couldn't imagine three years ago that I would be where I am today. I have Al-Anon and my Higher Power to thank for that. I lost my mother to this disease, and I almost lost my wife, but I have gained peace of mind and serenity.

Questions for reflection and meditation

- Am I still focused on finding help for the alcoholic in my life in a way that might take my focus off my own recovery?
- If I am caring for a chronically ill alcoholic, what are my own needs and how can I get them met?
- If there were a legitimate crisis occurring in my life today, what Al-Anon tools might help me deal with it constructively?
- In what ways have I ever created or contributed to a crisis situation?
- If there is a particular loss I fear will happen in the future, why does this potential loss attract my attention so strongly?

Loss of the Dream

"What I have lost is mainly an illusion of what I thought life would be."

We all have dreams, hopes, and plans for our future. One of the devastating effects of living with alcoholism is that our dreams for the future, for the lives we thought we would have, go unfulfilled. We may have looked forward to a long and happy life with our spouse or partner, only to have that dream shattered. A happy family life eluded many of us, and our children may have grown up amid chaos and even violence. Unresolved anger, grudges, or memories of abuse can divide our families and our friendships. Alcoholism can rob us of our dreams, and the magnitude of those losses can affect every aspect of our lives.

The losses that come from living with alcoholism often occur gradually and may differ from our other experiences with grief. At first, our losses may not be apparent to us. We may feel so confused by the dual nature of living with an alcoholic that, at times, we don't know what to think.

"The relationship I had with my husband—when he was sober—was loving, kind, and full of good memories of times shared. The relationship I had with my husband—when he was under the influence of alcohol—was sick and hurtful."

In the past when things didn't go our way, we told ourselves we needed to try harder or do better. We had yet to realize that our efforts at controlling were causing us more pain. In fact, many of us are surprised to find that our attempts at changing the alcoholic contributed to the problem, rather than to the solution. In trying so hard to make things turn out the way we wanted, we left little room for our Higher Power to work in our lives. We hoped for so long that life with the alcoholic would improve, but trying to solve our problems by ourselves only left us feeling isolated and exhausted.

We came to Al-Anon because we still have hope for a better way of life. As one member eventually came to understand, "Today I can't afford to think about what might have been." Despite our disappointments, we can, in time, begin to build new dreams. Though we may not have the families we hoped for, we discover that we do have the power to change our own lives—starting today.

Mourning what was lost, grieving what never was

When we first come to Al-Anon, many of us question what has become of our lives. We may be clinging to past hopes and dreams, or to memories of the alcoholic before the drinking began. We may be reluctant to accept our losses, fearing that our grief will consume us if we acknowledge it. We may not have had the relationship we wanted nor were we treated in the ways we hoped or expected. To cope with our pain, we may have created a fantasy of the perfect family, the perfect childhood, the perfect relationship, or the perfect life.

There lies a delicate balance between avoiding our pain and giving ourselves time to deal with it. We don't want to circumvent our grief, nor do we want to force ourselves to confront it before we are ready. Much like a child who needs the comfort of a security blanket, we may need to hold on to our dreams until we become ready to face life without them. We wouldn't rip away the blanket, nor would we reprimand the child for needing it. We trust that, when feeling safe enough, the child will let go of it. We can afford ourselves this same compassion and understanding, trusting that when the time is right we will be ready to face our losses.

> *"In a meeting, I heard someone say, 'the answer to the pain is in the pain,' and I decided to let go of control and allow the grief and my Higher Power to take me wherever I was meant to go."*

When we reach this point of letting go, we can begin to see others for who they are, rather than who we hope they will become. With this acceptance can also come a profound sense of loss. Many of us didn't get the lives we hoped for, but obsessing about what we perceive to be life's unfairness only sets us up for more misery. Eventually we learn to accept what is, even if it's not the way we would like it to be.

> *"In Al-Anon no one tried to help restore my lost dreams.*
> *Miraculously, I found that while I could not change the*
> *course of my family history, I had the strength and support*
> *of my program to allow me to rebuild a new and far richer*
> *life for myself than I ever could have planned or dreamed."*

Grieving for our children

Most parents want their children to grow up in a calm, nurturing, and loving home. Most often, however, our best intentions for creating this sort of environment couldn't prevent our children from being affected by the disease of alcoholism. We may have tried to perform the roles of both parents to make up for the alcoholic's lack of involvement or inability to be emotionally or physically present in our children's lives. We may have believed that if we tried hard enough, we could spare our children. Today we may be suffering from an overwhelming sense of guilt and regret at our inability to protect them from the alcoholic. Why, we wonder, didn't our efforts make a difference?

The fighting, violence, and instability in many alcoholic homes can affect our children well into their adulthood. Our children may have witnessed things we never imagined they would, and our dreams for raising them in a healthy and safe environment went unfulfilled. Some of us may have relied on our children to give us the emotional support and comfort we longed for from our alcoholic spouse. Now that we understand this was not their job, we may wish we could go back and do things differently.

Compassion for ourselves is critical as we examine this painful aspect of our past. Most of us did the best we could at the time with the knowledge and resources we had. With our new understanding, we can choose to focus on what we can do differently today. If we are currently living with violence, we can decide what action to take to protect our children and ensure their safety and our own. If our adult children are just beginning to come to terms with the effects of growing up in an alcoholic home, we may be confronted about our role and asked to relive painful moments from their childhoods. Though this can be a difficult time for us, we can do our best to offer them emotional support.

Applying the Fourth and Fifth Steps to our relationships with our children has helped many of us. The purpose of these Steps is not to blame ourselves, but rather to examine those aspects of our parenting where we made mistakes or caused harm. In Step Four, we make "a searching and fearless moral inventory of ourselves." In our inventory, we remember to acknowledge those aspects of our parenting we are proud of, as well as those aspects we regret. Our goal is to see ourselves accurately and to do what we can to repair our relationships with our children. When we are ready, we can make amends. While our children may not have had the childhoods we wanted or dreamed for them, it's not too late to do our part to build healthy relationships with them today.

Coming to terms with our unmet expectations

A dream is an aspiration, something we value, strive for, and work to achieve. An expectation has more to do with our state of mind and what we believe we deserve. Often our dreams and expectations are interwoven, and it can be difficult to tell them apart. Sometimes our expectations are reasonable, and sometimes they are unrealistic. For instance, we can reasonably expect that the sun will rise in the morning and set in the evening. If our oven is working properly, we can expect that when preheated, it will reach the desired temperature. In a healthy relationship, we can reasonably expect that we will be treated with the same dignity, consideration, and respect that we give others. When living with the chaos and unpredictability of alcoholism, however, even our most reasonable expectations often go unmet.

At a rational level, we may know all too well how unrealistic it is to expect someone who is drunk to consider us with respect, or to consider us at all. At an emotional level, however, we may feel surprised and repeatedly hurt whenever we are let down. If we've become accustomed to alcoholic behavior, we may start to believe we deserve nothing better. We may even begin to put ourselves down or to tolerate abuse from other family members, friends, or coworkers.

Just because someone is incapable of treating us with respect doesn't mean we aren't worthy of it. In Al-Anon we discover that *we* are the ones most capable of taking care of ourselves. This may be a jolting revelation to those of us who believed or were taught otherwise. Slowly we begin to reclaim our sense of self-worth. In time we discover that we are stronger and more resilient than we sometimes give ourselves credit for. By taking responsibility for our own lives, we begin to recognize that our happiness isn't contingent upon what others do or don't do. As we begin to reclaim our sense of self-worth, we will be more likely to attract healthier relationships based on mutual respect and consideration.

> *"Al-Anon gave me the tools to live my life with a deeper understanding of the many issues over which I am powerless. It also revealed to me the simple truth that I am in charge of my own happiness."*

When we apply our slogan "Let It Begin with Me," we stop waiting for others to meet our needs and instead look to ourselves. This does not mean we have to "do it all," or that we can't count on anyone. Rather, we learn to stop expecting our needs to be met by someone who is incapable of doing so. We can feel disappointed and let down without our whole world falling to pieces.

> *"If someone can't be a loving witness to my sadness, I can learn to accept it without resentment. Step Three helps me*

do this. When I think something isn't right in my world,
I remind myself that I turned my will and my life over to
the care of a loving Higher Power this morning. Even if my
expectations are not met, I am still safe."

At some point, we may need to examine whether we are allowing our expectations to control us. We can ask ourselves: Are we
overly attached to a particular outcome? Do we feel angry and
wronged if things don't turn out the way we had anticipated? Have
we been clinging too tightly to our plans, or are we able to hang
on loosely, with a willingness to adjust to new information as it
comes our way? Small disappointments, such as a last minute can-
cellation or being stood up by an alcoholic, can be over-amplified.
Such letdowns can be so upsetting because they often remind us
of our greater disappointments.

Daily contact with our Higher Power is important as we learn to
adjust our expectations. Step Eleven talks about praying *only* for
knowledge of God's will for us and the power to carry that out. The
word "only" serves as a reminder to take our will out of the equation.
Forcing our will has led to repeated disappointment for most of us.
What a relief it can be to trust that we will be given the strength
and resources necessary to carry out the will of our Higher Power.
Step Eleven does not promise a quick fix, however. Throughout
the day, we may need to surrender our will repeatedly. This can be
especially true while struggling to let go of expectations.

How do we recognize the will of our Higher Power? Many of us
become aware of our Higher Power in those still, quiet moments
during prayer or meditation when our minds are clear and free
from distraction. Some of us experience it as intuition—a quiet
but strong sense of knowing. Others describe it as inner peace
and resolve.

Daily contact with a Higher Power will look different for each
of us. If we belong to a particular religion, we may recite prayers
from our tradition. If we connect with our Higher Power through

nature, we make time for a walk in the woods, on the beach, or in our neighborhood. We can repeat the Serenity Prayer throughout the day or read from our literature. Making time for meditation each morning or evening can help quiet our minds. We can choose whatever works best for us to connect with our Higher Power. We don't have to do it perfectly. All we need to do is become willing.

Facing financial loss

We may have never dreamed we would be facing both alcoholism and financial hardship simultaneously, but the truth is that these two losses often go hand in hand. The alcoholic may be irresponsible with money, neglecting to pay the bills, rent, or mortgage; hiding money; or spending our entire savings without our knowledge. We ourselves may have turned to spending during stressful times. To compensate for the loss of affection and attention from the alcoholic, we may have looked to tangible pleasures to fulfill us. Since nothing can ever completely make up for the loss in our relationship, we can quickly find ourselves in a financial mess, trying to manage credit card debt or overdraft bank fees on top of everything else.

While many treatment programs and therapy centers can be costly, in Al-Anon we have no fees for attending meetings. This can come as a welcome relief to those among us who are struggling financially. Tradition Seven states that "every Al-Anon group ought to be fully self-supporting, declining outside contributions."

> *"Tradition Seven helped me see that I could become self-supporting instead of relying on the alcoholic to support me. My use of the slogans such as 'First Things First' and 'How Important Is It?' helped me prioritize my bills and learn to distinguish my wants from my needs. I now realize that no amount of things can replace the loss of my marriage."*

Although none of us wants to have to deal with a significant financial hardship, the enormity of such a problem can often force us to take a stand for ourselves and to set boundaries. One member almost lost her home because her husband neglected to pay their mortgage. She finally found the courage to tell him how his decisions were affecting her, and that if he didn't get treatment, she would leave the relationship. In Al-Anon we learn to mean what we say and say what we mean without having to be mean when we say it. We can voice the reality of a situation without resorting to manipulation. If we have made idle threats in the past, we'll need to consider whether we're prepared to follow through before we take this kind of stand. We may have once felt trapped in our marriages, our families, or our ways of life by our financial situations. In Al-Anon we discover that we have choices, and that making better financial decisions for ourselves today can help change the course of our lives.

We take care of ourselves financially by accepting our current situation and taking steps toward improving it. If our financial circumstances feel overwhelming, we can ask our Higher Power for help in managing our affairs. We might look to outside help if our money problems are beyond our ability to resolve on our own. Though it's difficult to stay in the present when we are struggling financially, we try not to project too far into the future. We focus on what we can do—right here, right now—to help better ourselves financially.

Loss of self-awareness

Perhaps one of the most tragic losses we will face as a result of living with alcoholism is loss of our sense of self. Constant focus on the alcoholic left many of us with little time or energy to know ourselves and who we really are. Furthermore, we may have spent years suppressing, minimizing, or ignoring our feelings or having our feelings disregarded by the alcoholic. If we stated our needs, we may have been told we were being selfish. Those of us who have lived with the threat of verbal, emotional, or physical abuse may have become accustomed to not speaking up for ourselves out of fear for our safety or the safety of our children. As time goes on, who we are gets buried beneath years of denial, neglect, and abuse. At meetings we hear others talk about taking care of themselves, but we may not know where to start. We may feel so disconnected from ourselves that if someone were to ask us what we needed, we wouldn't even know how to respond.

A good place for us to start is simply with the recognition that we have been putting ourselves last for too long. We can make a commitment to ourselves today that we will strive to take better care of ourselves, one day and one step at a time. Much like getting to know a new friend, we can make time to get to know ourselves. This can be a time of great freedom, and a time when we give ourselves permission to try new things. For instance, we may have always been afraid of going places alone, so we might try going to the movies or out to dinner by ourselves. As we explore new territory, we discover our likes and dislikes.

One member, while preparing to clean his fishbowl, filled the bathtub with water, removed the fish from the bowl, and placed them in the tub. Curious to see how the fish would respond to their new, vast environment, he stayed for a few moments to watch. To his surprise, the fish simply circled in the same amount of space their bowl provided. They had become so adapted to their old environment, they didn't realize they now had more room to swim.

Before Al-Anon, our lives may have felt as confining as a fishbowl. Like these fish, we too adapted to the limitations of our lives, unaware of another way. When we first come to Al-Anon, we realize that the world is much larger than a fishbowl. It might feel scary at first to be in unknown waters. As we let go of our old, familiar patterns, we become free to inhabit life—in all its vastness—more fully.

This period of freedom and self-discovery can be an opportune time to build or renew our relationship with a Higher Power. Even if we don't feel loved by anyone else, we can learn to trust that we are loved unconditionally by a Power greater than ourselves. Whenever we ask for help, our Higher Power will be there for us. One way our Higher Power reaches out to us is through the Al-Anon fellowship.

> *"I not only allowed my Higher Power to love me; I also allowed others in the program to love me. Having others believe in me before I was able to believe in myself brought new hope to my life."*

If we are struggling with loving and caring for ourselves, we can "act as if" for a while. Perhaps there is a member of our group whom we admire—whether our Sponsor or someone else. We might let this person serve as an example as we take the first tentative steps toward taking care of ourselves. The collective wisdom of our members can provide us with support and encouragement as we begin the journey toward reclaiming our lives.

The more we apply the Al-Anon ideas, the more changes we will see in ourselves. Along with these new and exciting changes may also come a sense of loss: Loss of our old selves, our old belief systems, our old ways of living, and sometimes our old relationships. It may seem strange to grieve for the parts of ourselves that led us to treat ourselves so poorly; but change—even good change—can trigger loss. Letting go is difficult, even when what we're letting go of is unhealthy or undesirable.

> *"Through this process of growth, I buried my old ways of thinking and the ways I treated myself. It felt much like burying old clothes that no longer fit me."*

Certain beliefs and behaviors must die in order for us to change. Once we're ready to let go of these aspects of ourselves, we turn to Step Seven. In this Step, we humbly ask our Higher Power to remove our shortcomings. Many of us have experienced a feeling of release when we request our Higher Power's help. As we let go of our old selves, we make room for the new. After divorce, one member felt suicidal: "Then I realized it wasn't *me*, but part of my belief system that needed to die." Our old coping mechanisms got us through some tough times, and for that we can be grateful, but it's also okay to say goodbye to those parts of ourselves.

Al-Anon may not be able to give us back everything we have lost, but it can restore our sense of hope. By learning to focus on ourselves, we find that peace and contentment are possible, even in the midst of uncertainty. As we gain strength and self-confidence, we find that we have loosened our grip on the dreams we once held so tightly. Before long, we realize we're building new dreams. An excerpt from Al-Anon's *Just for Today* bookmark reads: "Just for today I will adjust myself to what is, and not try to adjust everything to my own desires." We may always feel a certain degree of sadness for the loss of our dreams.

"An occasional glance over my shoulder is all right. It shows me how far I've come and how much I don't want to go back there."

Members share experience, strength, and hope: Loss of the dream

I longed for a perfect family all my life, one that was both loving and caring. In my imagination, I created this ideal family inspired by the fairy tales from my childhood. My real family turned out to be far different from my fairy-tale family. I did not marry Prince Charming and I do not have a Fairy Godmother. Not only are my children not close; at times, they don't even speak to one another. Sometimes we don't see each other on holidays or special occasions.

Working the Twelve Steps, especially Steps One through Three, has helped me understand that I am powerless over my family, and that I can't force us to love one another. I decided to share my fairy-tale family dream with God, placing that dream in His hands. I then asked God to make us the family *He* wanted us to be, instead of the family *I* wanted us to be. Letting go of that unrealistic dream and allowing God to be in charge freed me from my sense of responsibility for the success or failure of my family. What a great relief! Although we may never be a fairy-tale family, by turning my will and my life over to God as I understand Him, we may indeed live happily after all.

Before Al-Anon, I saw myself as someone who could handle whatever happened without complaining. After all, I was burdened with an alcoholic wife and I did all the work to support us. All the while, I put on a brave front that everything was fine at home. Once I started working the Al-Anon program, I discovered that I wasn't really all that noble. In many ways, I reacted to life just as the alcoholic did: I dealt with unpleasant situations by running away; I manipulated people and situations to fit my wants; and worst of all, I lied to myself.

It was unpleasant, to say the least, to realize that I had spent over 40 years believing I was a certain type of person, only to learn that I wasn't. It was almost as though I didn't exist. I've had to grieve for the loss of the image I had of that noble person who stood on mountaintops withstanding any storm without a whimper. Al-Anon has shown me that it's okay to grieve for the loss of the person I once thought I was. Those coping mechanisms were all I knew, and they got me through some tough times.

With the Al-Anon tools, I'm learning new ways of coping. As I build a new self-image, I can start to bid farewell to those parts of myself that are no longer useful. The new me is still flawed, but I'm aware of the flaws. Today I know that my Higher Power doesn't expect me to be perfect—only to keep moving forward as best I can.

When I got real with the help of Al-Anon, I had to admit that the perfect family I had dreamed of was not to be. My husband of more than 30 years was an alcoholic, and each of our four children had issues with him. Denial had prevented me from understanding my children and recognizing what alcoholism was doing to them.

As I take care of myself and work on my recovery, I am better able to support my children today. I encourage them to learn about the disease of alcoholism and how it has affected their lives. Improving my relationships with my children is my focus for today. The reality is bittersweet compared with the dream I had, but then I remember it was just that—a dream. Al-Anon helps me to focus on what is real and present in my life today and to look toward tomorrow with hope.

I grew up in an alcoholic home and moved out at 19. At 30, I married a wonderful man. Within six months, I realized he was an alcoholic. My pride dictated that I would make this marriage work. After waiting this long to marry, how could I admit I had made a mistake?

I had believed we would one day have children, but as my husband's drinking quickly escalated, my frightening childhood memories returned. I knew I was unwilling to bring a child into a home such as ours. I didn't have the courage to talk about this with my husband, so I avoided the topic altogether. Shortly after joining Al-Anon, however, I realized I would have to face my husband with my decision. With my newfound courage, I told him of my reasons and fears. He didn't receive it well, but I stuck to my decision. Reluctantly he finally agreed.

Years passed. Sobriety came into our home and I'm now retired. Still, at times, the unexpected yearning for children is overwhelming. I watch young parents with their babies, and I yearn to hold and cuddle them. I watch families celebrating special occasions and I feel such sadness. I watch others with their adult children and know I won't have that pleasure. Al-Anon reminds me that it's okay to mourn the loss of my dream for children. The grief over what I will never have is profound, even though I know that the decision I made many years ago was not a mistake.

My Higher Power has given me the gift of nieces and nephews and the adult children of my friends. My husband, siblings, and Al-Anon family also help fill the void. For these relationships, I am grateful. I may not have what I want, but I trust I have what I need.

———————————

I have often been disappointed in myself, others, and in circumstances that I have neither wanted nor anticipated. In the years since I've been recovering from the effects of alcoholism, I have stopped believing that life is either good or bad, or fair or unfair. Today I believe that life is bittersweet, and that the choices I make are either effective or ineffective.

It has been excruciatingly difficult and painful for me to realize that the life I had planned and expected never became a reality. My hopes and dreams did not materialize. Before Al-Anon, when my expectations were not being met, I thought I had to try harder or try to force myself and others to do and be what I wanted. It never once occurred to me that I could stop forcing solutions, or that my control was an illusion. Over the years, I have come up against insurmountable situations where the only choice I was left with was to grieve the loss of my expectations.

In the pursuit of trying to make my life happen according to my expectations, I overlooked the will of my Higher Power. I continue to discover old beliefs and expectations that cause me great suffering. When I allow myself to feel the loss of a relationship, hope, or dream, I enter the deepest form of prayer I know by grieving the death of what I believed was so important in my life. When I become willing to turn my will and life over to the care of God as I understand Him/Her, I empty myself of expectations and prepare to wait and anticipate God's will for me. God has much better access to my heart when it is open to inspiration, guidance, and acceptance.

I am extremely grateful to Al-Anon and the Twelve Steps for bringing me slowly out of unrealistic expectations into a life of meaning.

Questions for reflection and meditation

- How is my life different from what I had hoped for as a child? What can I still change and what do I have to accept?
- Have I considered how my response to the alcoholic situation has affected my children?
- Am I ready to forgive myself for the mistakes I made as a parent?
- What is my usual attitude when something in my life goes in a direction I didn't plan or anticipate?
- Is there a part of my old self or an old belief system that now gives me an opportunity to let go of something?
- What new dreams are possible for me today?

Grieving for Our Childhood

*"I have carried an immense grief since
childhood, but didn't know why."*

For those of us who grew up with alcoholism, the damaging effects of the disease can follow us throughout our lives. As children, we didn't have the emotional awareness to cope with the grief of growing up in an alcoholic home. Most of us were too busy surviving to be able to face our losses. We relied on our parents to provide us with a stable and safe environment, but they were often unable to do so. We were truly powerless to change our circumstances.

Having grown up with alcoholism, we may have been affected emotionally, psychologically, spiritually, and physically. As adults, we often struggle with fear, anxiety, or depression. Many of us first come to Al-Anon when we realize how the behaviors that once helped us survive have become a burden. They have gotten in our way and kept us from having the lives we want. If we've been running from our pain, we may feel ill-equipped to handle our emotions or face our painful memories. By keeping silent, we may unconsciously be keeping the family secret of alcoholism alive and well.

Keeping secrets is common in most alcoholic households. Many of us unknowingly honored an unspoken pact to keep quiet about what was going on at home. No wonder it can be so difficult later on to learn a new way of life. These secrets only fueled our sense of shame. When we were new to Al-Anon, we may have felt conflicted about whether to speak of the secrets we had kept for so long.

　　*"Al-Anon meetings became a place for me to have a voice for all
　　I had lost."*

In Al-Anon we find hope for a new way of life. As we come to understand alcoholism as a family disease, we can identify the behaviors that once helped us cope. Al-Anon offers us a safe haven where we can begin to talk openly about our past. Within such a warm and supportive environment, many of us can begin to take the first difficult steps toward facing the pain and loss from our childhoods. Though it may not seem possible, in time we can find compassion for ourselves, our family members, and even the alcoholic.

Growing up with active alcoholism

Some of us who came from alcoholic homes feel that we grew up too fast. We carried a burden of responsibility that was too much for any child to bear. The mood of the alcoholic often became the center of our lives, determining whether we had a good or bad day. Each of us had different coping mechanisms. Some tried to be the best child possible, believing we could prevent the alcoholic from drinking, even if just for one night. Others coped by rebelling or acting out. This may have been the only way we knew to get attention, even if that attention was negative. Because alcoholism is a family disease, we may also have been affected by our non-alcoholic parent, siblings, or extended family members.

Some of us grew up with parents who were emotionally or physically absent, while others grew up with physical violence and verbal abuse. Some of us were sexually abused. Still others became our parents' caretakers. We may have become so accustomed to living this way that we didn't even know something was wrong. Others recognized early on that something was wrong, but didn't know what to call it or how to change it.

As children, focusing on the alcoholic and other family members helped us survive. As adults, we struggle with keeping the focus on ourselves. We may question our intuition and our ability to make good, sound decisions—whether we're choosing what we want to do with our lives or what to order at a restaurant.

If we lived with violence in our homes, we may have learned that the best way to protect ourselves was by hiding or withdrawing. As adults, we may believe we have to hide certain parts of ourselves in order to be accepted or loved.

If we were in the role of defending or protecting other family members, we may have an overdeveloped sense of responsibility for those around us. Blaming ourselves for the alcoholic's behavior can weaken our self-esteem and lead us to believe that every conflict is our fault. Likewise, if we assume that others are out to hurt us, we might habitually guard ourselves against real or imagined threats.

"I felt personally responsible for everyone's unacceptable behavior."

Often the coping mechanisms we learned as children in order to survive get in the way of our developing meaningful and trusting relationships as adults. Identifying how we were affected by alcoholism is not about blaming the alcoholic or other family members for all our problems. Rather, it's about taking responsibility for our struggles so we can begin to heal. As children, we may not have had the power to change our circumstances. Now that we are adults, we can make that decision for ourselves.

Freedom to feel

Growing up, many of us were not free to express our feelings. Often the only person who was allowed to be angry was the alcoholic. As a result, we may have come to believe that certain feelings were wrong, and so we may have turned them inward. In Al-Anon we are allowed to feel our feelings, whatever they may be, without shame or guilt. Now that it is safe to express our feelings, we may be surprised to discover the depth of our emotions. Even the recollection of happy times can make us sad, for often those happy times were all too fleeting.

When we first begin recovery, we may struggle with our anger and resentment for the abuses we suffered as children. Though ultimately our healing is not about blaming our parents, we may need to get angry for a while. Some decide to confront their parents, while others choose not to. Some choose to remain in relationships with family members while they work on their recovery. Some find it best to limit the time spent with their families until they feel more confident in taking care of themselves. Others feel it is best to take time away from family altogether. There is no right or wrong way to deal with our families, and only we know what's best for us. Perhaps what's most important is to recognize that we have choices.

Though feeling our anger may make us uncomfortable, we can trust that it is an important facet of our grief and recovery. When we allow ourselves to experience the full range of our feelings, we come to realize that our anger can serve us in important ways. It lets us know when we've been hurt or mistreated or when someone has crossed a boundary. It might be signaling us to respond differently to a particular person or situation. Often our anger can be a reminder that we need to take better care of ourselves.

We may always be affected to some degree by our past, but we find that as we face our pain, it begins to lose its power. It might help to consider the following analogy: While driving a car, we glance in the rearview mirror to see what is happening behind us. We wouldn't want to stare in the mirror for too long, because this would be dangerous and could cause an accident. On the other hand, it would also be dangerous if we never looked in the mirror.

When it comes to our past, we can learn to find that delicate balance between looking and not looking. It takes time to let go. We can trust that our Higher Power will guide us through our grief at the pace that is right for us. The more we heal from our grief, the less we will feel the need to stare at it. In time many of us have been able to look at our past in a way that informs us rather than holds us hostage.

Dealing with abuse and violence from our past

Many of us who grew up in alcoholic homes were the victims of domestic violence. We witnessed things no child should ever have to see. We may have been physically, sexually, or verbally abused ourselves, or a parent or sibling may have been abused. Even if the alcoholic never laid a hand on us, witnessing a violent act can often be as traumatic as being the direct victim of it. We learned to read facial expressions, the weight of footsteps, and other unspoken signals. We became adept at discerning when to stay out of the way, or when a fight or violent episode was about to erupt.

While this degree of emotional sensitivity can be a desirable attribute—allowing us to feel empathy and compassion for others—it can also affect us negatively. We may react to situations and people based on impulse rather than evidence. Or we become like chameleons, constantly adapting or hiding parts of ourselves to suit the needs of others. If we learned to ignore our own needs, our tendency might be to abandon ourselves in our relationships or to choose people who are emotionally unavailable.

Living with violence on a daily basis has an effect that goes well beyond our childhood, and the cycle of abuse can cut across generations. Even though we told ourselves we never would, some of us end up marrying an alcoholic, becoming involved in violent relationships, or inflicting the same abuses we experienced upon our children or other loved ones. Regardless of whether we are currently involved in an abusive relationship, Al-Anon can help as we learn to break this destructive cycle.

Recovering from some abuses can take more time than we anticipate. We may find that we need to talk about certain traumatic events repeatedly. If we don't already have a relationship with a Sponsor, it can be especially helpful to develop one at this time. While it can help to share our story at meetings, a Sponsor can invest in-depth one-on-one time with us and listen in more detail.

That person can help us be accountable for working our program and can guide us if we feel lost or overwhelmed. However, it is important to remember that some issues are so deep that they may warrant professional help in addition to the caring support of Al-Anon members.

> *"Our Suggested Welcome says that we are not alone. Hearing that at each meeting comforts me. I am no longer that small child hiding behind the sofa."*

Our relationship to our childhood wounds can change as we recover. In time we may find that we no longer identify ourselves solely with our past abuses. Rather, we learn to live with our past without allowing it to define us. As we begin to practice the principles of the program, we may find that we are no longer attracted to abusive relationships. Instead, we are drawn to people who treat us with the love and respect we've always deserved.

Accepting the families we had

Even if certain family members are still living, many of us feel as if we are already mourning their loss. We grieve for loss of the relationships we wanted but couldn't have because of the disease of alcoholism.

> *"When my father died of alcoholism, not only did I grieve his death, but also his life. I grieved for my childhood that was lost to parenting my dad. I grieved for the man he could have been. How could I miss a father I never had?"*

Al-Anon can help us see that even though we may wish we could change our families, it's not in our power to do so. Accepting the families we had doesn't mean we excuse past abuse. Nor does it mean we ignore or tolerate any present abuse either. Expecting our families to give us something they don't have is like hoping to fill a water bucket from an empty well. Hoping that "this time things will be different" is one way we keep our grief at a distance.

"Al-Anon taught me to be for myself what I wanted from others.
That was an amazing concept for someone whose mood
changed with the mood of her alcoholic parents."

It can be difficult to let go of our dream for the family we wanted. But in doing so, we learn to see our families accurately—the negatives *and* the positives. We stop expecting them to be other than who they are. Acceptance may not always feel good, but it can free us from the burden of our old expectations.

Once we reach this level of acceptance with our families, we become free to welcome other people into our lives who can be there for us in ways our families can't. Some of us refer to such people as our "family of choice." For many of us, our family of choice includes Al-Anon members.

"My Sponsor gave me the unconditional love I had always
needed. She told me how well I was doing and that she
was amazed and in awe of how much I was growing in the
program. She told me how much she loved me. Through
my Sponsor, God provided me with the love I needed but
didn't get from my mother."

Though we may have come to a deeper understanding about our families, we can still give ourselves permission to take care of ourselves when we are with them. Detaching can be critical to our own mental, physical, or spiritual well-being. At first, we may not know how to detach gracefully. As we come to understand more about detaching with love, we learn the difference between building walls and setting limits. If our primary goal is to heal our relationships, we keep striving to find healthy ways to relate to our families, while still respecting ourselves.

Forgiving our families

Some of us may have convinced ourselves that we should forgive others based solely on certain religious beliefs or cultural traditions. Genuine forgiveness is not something we arrive at easily. It doesn't mean we forgive out of fear or obligation, or to keep peace in our relationships.

Forgiveness does not mean we forget about the past. Nor does it mean we accept repeated mistreatments. After all, many of us have learned valuable lessons from our past that helped shape who we are today. Eventually, however, the burden of carrying around our pain can take its toll on us. If we're finding it hard to forgive, we might still be in pain. If this is the case, we might benefit from allowing ourselves more time to heal before we even begin to think about forgiveness.

Ultimately forgiveness is an action we take to free ourselves from the pain we've been carrying. Forgiveness creates space in our lives for our own healing. In fact, forgiveness can be an important step in taking care of ourselves. We can forgive and rebuild our damaged relationships, or we can forgive and still choose to distance ourselves from certain people who continue to be abusive.

When we think about forgiveness, we also consider those mistakes we have made for which we'd like to make amends. Perhaps we have neglected to see our parents as people with their own challenges. After all, many of our parents grew up in alcoholic homes too, having faced many of the same experiences we faced. Or perhaps we've been clinging to our resentments. If we've been emotionally withholding in an effort to punish someone else for their past mistakes, we may have amends to make.

Having empathy for our parents' struggles doesn't mean we excuse or accept abusive behavior. When it comes to forgiveness, we can love someone and still hold them accountable for their behavior. We can have compassion for the alcoholic and other family members even if we hate the effects of the disease of alcoholism on our lives.

Al-Anon as family

The concept of family tends to evoke strong responses from most people. Upon hearing the word "family," we may feel an overwhelming sense of security and connection, or tremendous sadness and pain. When we are with our families, we may feel loved and accepted, or displaced and alone. By definition, a family is a group of people bound together through shared ancestry. When we broaden our view of ancestry to include shared experience, we come to understand that family is not just limited to blood relations. Fortunately for many of us, we don't have a genetic connection to be part of a family.

"After shedding many tears—convinced that my prayers for a close family would go unanswered—I came to realize that families come in many forms. I know now that my real family is comprised of program people. They are the ones who celebrate milestones with me, who hold my hand during the tough times, and who encourage my growth. Though I'm not totally free of the heartbreak of not having the family I longed for all these years, I'm so grateful to know that I am part of the Al-Anon family."

We are called Al-Anon Family Groups for a reason. Though we may not share the same history or memories, we come together because we are bound by our shared experience of living with the effects of alcoholism. For many of us, the honest sharing among Al-Anon members often becomes the impetus for deep and lasting friendships. Because we feel accepted and loved unconditionally in Al-Anon, many of us have come to think of our group as our family. Just as any relationship requires nurturing, so too do our Al-Anon relationships. By attending meetings on a regular basis and spending time with other members outside meetings, we get to know those in our group, and they get to know us.

Holidays can be particularly difficult when it comes to dealing with the loss of our families. We might imagine that others have ideal holidays, that everyone gets along, and that the whole family gathers around the piano while a fire that no one seems to tend crackles in the background. We have seen this fantasy portrayed repeatedly on television and in movies. Though we know better, we may still find ourselves desiring this illusive way of life.

> *"I once heard 'these pictures only last for two minutes—any family can look good for that period of time.' It allowed me to let go of that perfect moment dream."*

Nostalgia and sentiment can often cloud our thinking. We may try to recreate the good memories we once had, hoping that this year, things will be different. Unless the situation within our families has improved, chances are, things will not be different. Each year, we usually end up feeling the same—disappointed and let down.

As we change, we find that our expectations of our families will also change. This doesn't mean we no longer have to take care of ourselves or set boundaries. If we choose to spend time with our families on holidays, we can plan ahead to assure we get the support we need. If we know we're going to be out of town, we can go to extra meetings before we leave or take phone numbers of our Sponsor and other Al-Anon friends with us. If things feel tense when we are with our families, we can take a break by stepping outside to get some fresh air, going for a walk, or even finding a meeting.

So much of our recovery depends upon our changed attitudes. When we stop expecting the holidays to unfold in a certain way, we can recognize that we have choices about how to spend the day. Some of us find the holidays more enjoyable and less stressful when we spend them with close friends or our Al-Anon family instead of our relatives.

Members share experience, strength, and hope: Grieving for our childhood

Living with alcoholism was like living in a constant state of grief. I lost so much to the disease, including a portion of my childhood. I grew up too fast, lost my natural trust of others, and lost respect for my mother as she gave up all sense of self and any semblance of dignity to the bottle. I never felt close to her or truly loved.

I escaped my home life when I got married and moved out at 17. My marriage ended up being a great distraction from my mother's drinking. I couldn't be nearly as consumed with her drinking once I realized my husband had a drinking problem that was even worse than hers. As the drinking in my home progressed, I lost my hopes and dreams for the future and any chance for a "happily ever after."

I don't know how I found the Al-Anon program, but thank God I did. I learned a lot, primarily about the family disease of alcoholism, its power, and my powerlessness. This was one of the first things that helped to ease the pain. It also gave me a starting point, a place where I could step back and gain some perspective on my life. In the program, I learned to crawl before I could walk, and I crawled for a long time.

A key turning point in my growth began when I found a Sponsor. By having someone I was accountable to, I didn't have a whole lot of room for self-pity, self-righteousness, or self-justification. With her help, I began my journey through the Steps. Working Steps One through Three opened the doors of my mind and heart. But Steps Four through Nine were the ones that set me free—free of so much pain, anger, bitterness, and confusion. In doing so, I gained perspective about myself and my role in the insanity of alcoholism. I began to see my mother in an entirely new light. I was able to make direct amends to her and establish a close, loving relationship with her that I never had as a child. I limited my time with her while she was drinking, and I extended that time when she was sober.

Our relationship healed in a way I never thought possible, allowing us many precious moments together over several years. My mother died a few years ago, and the pain of losing her surpassed anything I ever could have expected. Ironically, I don't believe I would have suffered this degree of pain if it weren't for the program and my new relationship with her. Nevertheless, the peace, joy, love, and fellowship of Al-Anon and the relationships I have found there have sustained me through my grief. I know that no matter how bad or sad I feel, I can and will feel better if I go to a meeting, pick up the phone, or utilize one of our program tools. This way of life has taught me that I don't ever have to be alone again.

When my mother died, my feelings of devastation surprised me. The times I remember that she and I actually got along were few and far between. My mother molded me to be her replacement in our family. She worked long, hard hours to put food on the table, while my job was to make sure the house was clean and the children were taken care of. If anything went wrong, I was blamed. Unfortunately, she and I never got the chance to resolve and heal from our turbulent relationship.

My siblings quickly found a substitute for their own unresolved issues after Mom died: Me. This was a pattern firmly set in our childhood. Our whole family still suffered because of our father's alcoholism. Even though he had died long ago, we were all still locked in the grip of the disease. We had no boundaries. My siblings dealt with their own grief the only way they knew how—with slanderous behavior and verbal abuse toward me and my children. I fell into the depths of despair and loneliness. In an effort to move on with my life, I mentally "buried" my siblings along with my mother, and commenced a new life without them.

I found comfort in Al-Anon meetings just knowing that I was unconditionally loved and accepted. My Al-Anon family understood what I was going through, because they had gone through their own struggles. They helped me through the loneliness that accompanied my grief. Before Al-Anon, my life was full of confusion, torn apart, and left shattered by the disease of alcoholism. My mom's passing freed me to heal, move on, and focus on the life I have. Today I am able to see that my mom and dad were ordinary people who struggled with the disease of alcoholism.

Today old memories no longer dominate my life as they once did. I cannot change what was, but I can change me and embrace what life has to offer me today. No longer am I going to allow the disease of alcoholism to rob me of life's experiences.

I made a decision to back off from my family for a while in order to sort through my pain. My denial had been preventing me from seeing how we had all been deeply affected by this disease. My conversations and visits with family during that time were brief. I learned that my family was not capable of giving me the support and unconditional love I needed, and I grieved for my dream of the family I always wanted.

Al-Anon gave me other choices—to stop looking in the same place for different results and, instead, to find people who were capable of giving me what I needed. By going to meetings, Al-Anon conventions, Assemblies, and workshops, I was able to have a family in Al-Anon—one of unconditional love and respect. Members have loved me when I felt angry and did not know how to love myself. They've embraced me and shared my happiness and joys. They've taught me to love myself and others.

In Al-Anon I have found many new and awesome friendships. I have been able to let go of my illusions of the family dream and to embrace the family I do have. I can now visit my family more, enjoy being around them, and give them the gift of unconditional love, respect, and support that I have been so freely given in Al-Anon.

My mother died when I was nine, and my stepfather got legal custody of me. The year after she died, he began physically, sexually, and emotionally abusing me. For years I wanted to know why. Why had my mom given him so much control of me? I was so angry with her. I never left flowers on her grave.

After several years in Al-Anon, I returned home to visit my mother's gravesite. Standing there, the reality of her life hit me hard. She was the daughter of a violent alcoholic. She was 32 years old and had been dying of cancer since she was 27. She was a frightened, sick young woman caring for a young child. If not for Al-Anon, I would still feel anger and resentment toward her. Standing at her grave, I felt compassion for my mother and realized how her circumstances prevented her from making better decisions for me. In that moment, I realized that my mom and I were not so different. She had the family disease of alcoholism, just like me. I was able to forgive my mother for the decisions that had made life so hard for me. Before leaving, I placed a bouquet of flowers on her grave.

It's taken a long time for me to recognize that I was more affected by my mother than by the alcoholic in our home. With this realization comes a deep sense of loss for what could have been if my mother had found recovery. It's been three years since she died, and we didn't have the chance to repair our relationship.

My recovery in Al-Anon has had much to do with my mother. She was the reason I came to my first meeting. It's not that she introduced me to the program; rather, I realized I was beginning to behave like her. As a teenager, I made a pledge that I would never be like my mom, and here I was starting to act just like her! I saw myself as a victim. I had an explosive temper. When life wasn't going my way, I would scream and pout. I became depressed and exhausted after angry outbursts, and sleep became my escape.

With the help of Al-Anon, I have been able to see my mother

in a new light. When I realized that she was also affected by the disease of alcoholism (her grandfather and my step-dad were both alcoholics), I could feel compassion toward my mother. Today I am able to appreciate the gifts my mom has given me. She showed me how to be hospitable. She was smart, enjoyed learning new things, and loved exploring the world. When I look at who I am today, I see a picture of myself glowing with all the gifts I've received from both Al-Anon and my mom. And I am grateful.

Questions for reflection and meditation

- In what ways does my upbringing in an alcoholic home affect my attitudes about my family life today?
- What painful parts of my past do I prefer to avoid thinking about?
- Can I recognize within myself feelings of anger from the losses of growing up in an alcoholic home? What do these feelings of anger tell me about myself?
- What three simple things can I do to take better take care of myself the next time I am with my family of origin?
- What does forgiveness mean to me?
- What can the Serenity Prayer teach me about accepting my family for who they are and my hopes that they can still become more like the family I always wanted?
- Am I ready to rebuild a relationship with my parents or other family members?
- How does my concept of family hurt or help my sense of well-being?

Loss In Relationships

"Grieving the loss of a relationship is not unlike grieving a death."

Life is full of change. So too are our relationships. If we're lucky, a few relationships will last our entire lives. Some will last for years, others for months or weeks. Regardless of the duration, each of our relationships has much to teach us about ourselves and can help us see the areas where we'd like to grow or change.

The truth is, any change in our relationships can trigger loss. For instance, a longtime Sponsor may move out of town, or a favorite meeting we've been attending for years may end. We may divorce or separate from a spouse or significant other. We may decide to distance ourselves from an alcoholic parent, family member, friend, or our adult children, or they may distance themselves from us.

Most long-term relationships go through periodic struggles and changes. Even when a relationship continues, something may happen that will shift things permanently, impacting our lives in profound ways. Even if we continue to see our loved one on a regular basis, we can still feel a sense of loss.

Our work in Al-Anon is not just about healing ourselves; it's also about healing our relationships. The more time we spend in Al-Anon, the more comfortable we become with practicing new behaviors. We let go of trying to force solutions and start taking care of ourselves.

When we begin to recover, our relationships can change too. Some of our relationships will end because of our recovery. Sometimes we make the decision to leave a relationship, and sometimes the other person chooses to leave. However, some of us have been fortunate enough to see our relationships blossom and grow because of our recovery.

Should I leave or should I stay?

*"Though I was a strong leader and successful in my career,
my marriage was being claimed by my wife's alcoholism.*

I found myself a broken human being on the doorsteps
of Al-Anon. A friend assured me I would find help there.
I remembered Al-Anon as the 'woman's group' from my
childhood, but I soon found there was a place for men in
Al-Anon too."

Many of us decided to try Al-Anon when we realized that our best efforts at trying to improve our relationship with the alcoholic weren't working. Our distorted thinking may have convinced us that it was our job to show the alcoholic a better way of life. At first, we may have thought Al-Anon could give us some new ideas.

It didn't take long before we realized that Al-Anon was not about fixing the alcoholic. Initially we may have been reluctant to give up our old ways of thinking.

"I came into Al-Anon to fix my broken husband but was told
that I had to change. But if I let go of trying to fix him, what
else would I have? That's who I was—a victim of constant
pain! I relished that role and didn't want to give it up."

When considering whether to leave a relationship, many of us have found it beneficial to take a Fourth Step inventory. By facing our own defects of character, we come to recognize how our enabling and rescuing may have contributed to our unhealthy relationships. Sharing our insights with our Sponsor or a trusted Al-Anon friend helps us see those areas we'd like to change so we can avoid making the same mistakes in the future.

"After I began working the Steps, I recognized my own
complicity in our marital affairs."

Some of us decide to stay with the alcoholic. We may not be ready to leave or may not want to. If our loved one is ill, leaving the relationship may not feel like a viable option. We might decide to stay because we are hopeful that if we practice the Al-Anon principles, our relationship will improve. We might also choose to stay because the relationship has already improved—or even if it hasn't—because our attitude toward it has changed. Others arrive at the difficult decision to leave.

Al-Anon does not advocate any one decision when it comes to our relationships. Only we will know what is best for us. We can be free to make up our own minds, knowing we'll be supported no matter what we decide.

If we are unclear about what step to take, we can simply take some time to quiet our minds. Attending a meeting can offer tremendous relief. Being in the presence of people who are working toward building healthier lives can help us gain confidence and clarity. With the support of other members, we can find the strength to make decisions that once seemed insurmountable.

When we apply our slogan "Let It Begin with Me" to our relationships, we make a concerted effort to put the focus on ourselves. Instead of placing our lives on hold and waiting for others to change, we begin to see what we can do to improve our situation. The more we focus on ourselves, the better equipped we will be to handle whatever changes come our way in our relationships.

When the decision to leave is ours

Taking care of ourselves might mean making the difficult decision to end a relationship. It's not just marriage or partnerships we choose to leave. We may end relationships with certain friends, family members, and even our children. Although we may initiate the end of the relationship, and even if we feel no regrets, we can still expect to experience the same feelings of grief and loss that would arise if the decision were not ours.

Denial, guilt, and a lack of self-respect may have kept us in an unhealthy or abusive relationship with the alcoholic for years. While waiting for our relationship with the alcoholic to improve, we may have been anticipating a particular outcome.

*"The program helped me realize I could no longer expect my
husband to get sober so I could get on with my life. If I was
to have any life at all, I would have to change."*

Countless times we may have talked ourselves out of leaving,
replaying in our minds the various scenarios of disaster that
would happen if we did. We may fear that we won't be able to
survive without the alcoholic, or we may worry that the alcoholic
will spiral downward into a life of despair, chronic illness, or even
death if we leave. The alcoholic may blame us for ending the relationship, or we may assume the blame.

Some of us experience moments of regret over our decision
to leave a relationship, recalling the good times shared or over-
focusing on the positive attributes of the other person. We may
temporarily "forget" why we decided to end the relationship,
glossing over years of abuse, struggle, or loneliness. It can be helpful to remember that regret is often a part of grief. Just because we
feel regret doesn't mean we made a bad decision.

Some of our friendships may have worked prior to our recovery, but today we may find those relationships unfulfilling. This
is because we have changed. If we are fortunate, our friends and
loved ones will accept the changes they see in us. Sometimes
our recovery can be the catalyst for change in our relationships.
At other times, we discover that it's in our best interest to end
certain destructive relationships, and instead build new and
healthier ones.

When the decision to leave is not ours

Sometimes the decision to end a relationship is not up to us.
Not everyone will accept how we've changed, and some may question what has happened to the "old" us. We have been so focused
on everyone else for so long, others may even accuse us of being
selfish for tending to ourselves. Those who are unable or unwill-

ing to accept our recovery might choose to end their relationship with us.

Initially we may find it difficult to let ourselves believe that the relationship is over. We may be reluctant to move on, holding out hope for a reconciliation. If we hoped that our relationships would improve because of our recovery, we may have a hard time accepting that some of them will end. We may find ourselves obsessed with what might have been or what we could have done differently. If both people involved are willing, an open and honest discussion can help us understand how we may have contributed to any problems in the relationship. Introspection such as this allows us to learn from our mistakes and to apply what we've learned to our relationships in the future.

"Live and Let Live" reminds us that we cannot control the actions or decisions of other people. If someone chooses to end a relationship with us, that is their right. If we've ascribed to the belief that the success or failure of our relationships is solely our responsibility, we may blame ourselves when a relationship ends. We can remind ourselves that each person played a part in the relationship. If a relationship ends, that doesn't mean we're necessarily at fault. Whether or not someone wants to be around us, we are still worthy of love and respect.

Just because we didn't choose to end the relationship doesn't mean we don't have any choices. We still have the power to choose how we will respond. In the past, we may have punished ourselves or assumed our role as victims. We don't have to see ourselves as victims anymore. Today we can choose to be around healthy people who want to be around us.

Separation and divorce due to alcoholism

Alcoholism can rob us of the emotional, physical, and sexual intimacies essential to a healthy marriage or partnership. Most of us tried everything to get the alcoholic to stop drinking. We prayed, cried, threatened to leave, begged, and pleaded for them to find help. We may have stood by our alcoholic spouse or significant other through countless drunken episodes, and through years of verbal, emotional, or physical abuse. While we may have been devoted and dedicated to our relationship, the disease caused the alcoholic to be emotionally and physically unavailable.

After much heartbreak, many of us have come to accept that we can't fix our relationship all by ourselves. We recognize that living with alcoholism has taken its toll on us physically, emotionally, and spiritually. We may have never imagined we would find ourselves at the crossroads of divorce or separation, but here we are. Accepting that the relationship we once had no longer exists can be devastating. Most likely, however, we have been grieving for the loss of our relationship with the alcoholic long before it officially ended.

For those of us who are parents, we may not be able to fathom taking our children away from the alcoholic parent. We may worry that it would be too traumatic for them. For others, seeing the effects of alcoholism on our children prompted us to leave. Some of us arrive at the decision quickly, but others may struggle for years. Well-meaning individuals and even clergy members may have advised us not to leave the alcoholic. We don't have to let other people's opinions or moral and religious beliefs determine what decision we make. Taking the advice of others to heart has led too many of us to blame ourselves for breaking up our families, instead of recognizing that the disease of alcoholism was to blame.

The decision to divorce or separate can often be a decision to say yes to life. In the past, we may have put our lives on hold, hoping things would get better. If only the alcoholic would stop drinking, we may have convinced ourselves, then we could be happy. Al-Anon teaches us that we are responsible for our own lives and our own happiness. We may need to grieve for all the time we spent worrying and trying to control someone else. The good news is, we can now use that time for the benefit of ourselves.

Healing our relationships with our adult children

Whether or not the alcoholic finds sobriety, or whether or not we stay in the relationship, we still have to face the effects of alcoholism on our children. While they were young, we may have believed we could prevent our children's suffering by trying to compensate for the lack of attention they received from the alcoholic. Some of us tried to educate our children about alcoholism or urged them to attend Alateen. While these efforts may have helped, we couldn't prevent our children from being affected by the family disease of alcoholism.

The effects of growing up in an alcoholic home follow most children into their adulthood. They may suffer from anxiety, depression, and low self-esteem. Many have difficulty trusting other people. They may choose relationships with other alcoholics or struggle with their own addictions. As parents, we may have sent our teenage children to alcohol treatment centers, or had to ask them to leave our homes. We had to set limits and then find the courage to implement them.

In Al-Anon we learn that we cannot control the choices of our adult children. As parents, this can be especially difficult to accept. After all, when our children were young, we were responsible for their welfare, making decisions we believed were in their best interest. Once our children are grown, it can be challenging to let them make their own decisions, especially if we view those decisions as potentially unwise or harmful. This doesn't mean we ignore problems as they arise. We can still express our concerns if asked, but we don't have to solve every problem they encounter.

*"I am learning to let go of my concerns about my son's welfare
so that he can turn to his Higher Power for help."*

Our impulse to rescue our children may actually prevent them
from finding their own solutions. What we *can* do is turn our
children over to our Higher Power's care.

*"When my adult children aren't behaving as I think they
should, I try to remember to 'Live and Let Live.' When I
think they are in trouble, I remind myself that I can't fight
their battles for them. Though it's painful to see them
stumble, I must 'Let Go and Let God.' It's hard enough
for me to stay on my own path; one way I can honor my
children is by letting them walk theirs."*

It can be easy to blame ourselves for our children's problems,
especially once we become aware of the damaging effects of living
with alcoholism. We may question the job we did as parents, wondering if we didn't protect our children enough or protected them
too much; if we were too hard or too easy on them. Because we
spent so much time focusing on the alcoholic, we may wonder if
we devoted enough of our energy to our children. Our concerns
may be compounded if our children blame us for their problems.

Guilt over past mistakes can keep us trapped. It helps to have
compassion for ourselves and our children. Even if we made mistakes in the past, we didn't cause anyone to become an alcoholic,
including our adult children. We simply don't have that kind of
power. We can remember to forgive ourselves. We can accept that
we did the best we could at the time with the resources we had.
Today we can make a commitment to do things differently.

How can we be there for our children today? We can offer our
love, support, and encouragement. We can model a healthier way
of life. We can talk openly with them about the mistakes we made.
We can listen without getting defensive if they want to talk about
their childhoods. We can allow room for their feelings and experiences, even if we might see things differently.

Our children's lives may not have turned out the way we had hoped, but we can't prevent them from learning the lessons they are meant to learn today. Whatever problems they may be facing are theirs to face. They have their own path, their own journey. Though it may be unclear to us now, perhaps our children are meant to go through exactly what they are going through for a reason.

Members share experience, strength, and hope: Loss in relationships

I had been in the program for several years when my wife decided to leave me and our children so she could seek sobriety. Her leaving prompted me to take the First Step on our marriage. I accepted that it wasn't what I was pretending it was, and that it would never be what I wanted it to be. Real men do cry, and I cried over the loss of the illusion of my marriage. I talked about it with other Al-Anon members and shared at meetings. In the process, I vowed that I would never again live with active alcoholism. When my wife returned home several months later, I set a boundary that active alcoholism in our home was no longer something I would tolerate.

She remained sober for two years and then relapsed. The disease progressed rapidly. I knew that as long as we were together, my enabling her would prevent her from finding long-term sobriety. It was at this point that I acted on the boundary I had set. I initiated a divorce and sought full custody of our children. The night I made my decision, I read from our Conference Approved Literature on divorce, and I prayed and meditated with my Higher Power. I drafted a letter to my wife about my desire to seek a divorce. Before giving it to her, I shared it with my Sponsor to ensure that I was speaking with kindness and respect, and that I was properly articulating my role in the situation.

My grief was more intense while I was coming to terms with the illusions of my marriage than it was during the divorce. I believe this allowed me to be more available to my children as they faced their own difficulties in dealing with the divorce and their mother's disease.

I came to Al-Anon one week after my 30th wedding anniversary, which I could not bring myself to celebrate. I had decided that I could no longer cope with my spouse's alcoholism and could not stay in the marriage. My grief at the thought of ending our marriage and the loss of the love and dreams we once had was overwhelming. Facing the fact that the drinking was not going to stop—that we were not going to live happily ever after or even have a normal life together— seemed more than I could bear. I cried for weeks.

After this breaking point, I came to the conclusion that my spouse and I might benefit from some outside help. Neither of us had ever considered this because we lived in denial of our problems. I considered many options, one of which was Al-Anon. As luck would have it, the next day I saw someone I knew who was in the program. I found the courage to ask her about a meeting time and place. She brought me a newcomer packet the next day. I eagerly read the pamphlets and cried all the way through *Alcoholism, a Merry-Go-Round Named Denial.* My spouse and I had acted out every scenario mentioned at one time or another.

I was so scared and distraught during my first meeting. Admitting my problems aloud to strangers was difficult. My husband is still an active drinker, and we are still married. Recognizing that alcoholism is a disease allowed me to treat my spouse with respect instead of disdain. Today I know how to detach from nastiness and not react. I know my happiness doesn't depend on what others say or do. Best of all, I know that I didn't cause the disease, I can't cure it, and I can't control it. Going to that first Al-Anon meeting was the best thing I have ever done for myself. I believe Al-Anon saved my marriage and my life.

I came to Al-Anon to fix my marriage to an alcoholic. My husband had become very distant and cold, and though we lived in the same house, we led separate lives. I knew when I married him that he was an alcoholic, but I knew nothing about alcoholism. I believed he was cured because he didn't drink and told me he didn't need to go to meetings anymore. I justified his anger, blame, mood swings, and silence by thinking they were my fault. I felt responsible for everything that went wrong. If he said it was my fault, I accepted that. I truly loved this man with all my heart, and I was determined to make this marriage work. I did everything I could to try to understand what was wrong in our relationship. I already had one failed marriage, and I didn't want another.

Soon after coming to Al-Anon, I realized that I was not the person who could make my husband's life right, and he could not cure what was wrong with me. I found that happiness is an inside job, and the only one who could make him truly happy was him. The same was true for me. I began detaching and working the program, all the while hoping and praying that our marriage would improve.

A year later, my husband left me. I was devastated, but fortunately, my year in Al-Anon had prepared me for this. My relationship with my Higher Power helped me get through this difficult time. I still miss and love the person my ex-husband was, but I know that my life is in the hands of a Power greater than myself who is taking care of me today. As I work my program, I continue to get better as I learn to come to terms with my past.

I was offered a job in another state to do work that, although at times unknowingly, I had been preparing to do for over twenty-five years. It seemed like an easy decision, except for one aspect: If I accepted the job, I would be leaving my partner of 12 years—the love of my life and my soul mate. He would not be able to relocate due to his own job situation.

My partner and I had met in Al-Anon, and with the help of the program, we always encouraged each other to follow our hearts. But truthfully, my heart felt quite divided. I found it extremely difficult to leave my will out of the equation. I had been repeating the Third Step first thing each morning for years, saying that I was turning my will and life over to the care of the God of my understanding. Were these mere words? Did I really mean them? Could I let go of the outcome and trust my Higher Power?

I found myself relying heavily on the prayer and meditation referred to in the Eleventh Step, doing my best to listen to God's will. It didn't take long before the answer was clear. It was revealed to me in the simplest and apparently unrelated moments—a reading at an Al-Anon meeting, a song on the radio, a conversation recalled from long ago. Soon I knew, without a doubt, that I needed to accept the job. I also knew that love, if it is healthy and strong, is mightier and more resilient than distance or time. We both decided to remain together—in heart and spirit across the miles.

The ensuing grief has been taxing on us both. In my previous experiences with grief, it tended to diminish with time. Yet this grief has only grown stronger. Friends have said, "You must be getting used to it," but I'm not. I know that unlike those who have lost their spouses or partners to death, I'm privileged that I can speak with my partner every day and see him every few months. The rewarding work I am doing provides some balance to my grief and reminds me that despite the pain involved, I am a very fortunate man. Still, the pain of missing him affects me daily.

It's been over five years since I took the job and moved away, and there's no change in our situation. Yet Al-Anon reminds me that the same Power that guided us both in making our decision cares for us even in our grief. I still feel in my heart that my Higher

Power has placed us exactly where we are meant to be. Whenever I meditate about it, which is still quite often, I continue to receive a one-word answer: "Trust."

I remind myself to take life "One Day at a Time," and "Just for Today." Though I can't see the bigger picture, as my faith and trust grow, I find I have less of a need to see it. My life will work out in the way God intends, regardless of my intentions. Ongoing grief of this kind continues to be difficult, but with the spiritual help I get from Al-Anon, I do receive solace.

Even though my husband had found sobriety, our children started acting out in major ways during their teenage years. I ended up making the decision to send my 17-year-old son to an adult halfway house out of state, where he promptly got kicked out for continued alcoholic behavior. He was okay and staying with a friend, but I was not okay.

After many tears and talks with my Sponsor, she suggested that maybe I was grieving. I was startled by her suggestion, but after giving it some thought, I realized she was right. Not only had I "lost" my son physically, but many years of alcohol abuse had taken him away from me emotionally before I was ready. I began to admit to myself and share at meetings that I was grieving. This allowed me to begin to heal.

Of my son I used to say, "I didn't get to finish with him." What I meant is that he didn't go through the usual process of growing up, moving out, and moving on. He was torn out of his child-hood and away from home as the result of his behaviors. Now I know that as painful as all that was, it was what had to happen. In Al-Anon I heard stories much worse than mine. One friend had lost a son to death, and another had no idea where her son was for years. At least I could be grateful that I knew where my son was and that his Higher Power was keeping him safe. And yet my grief was still very real and I had to go through it as if he had died.

Today I know that Al-Anon is what saved me. My grief was made more bearable because I didn't have to go through it alone.

Though my own parents loved me and wanted the best for me, they had difficulty accepting I was gay. So when my partner's parents welcomed me as part of their family, I found the acceptance I never got from my own. Over the years, we've built a very close relationship. The announcement of my partner's mother's Alzheimer's came as a blow. I felt like this wonderful woman had just come into my life, and now she was being taken out of it.

I use the principles I've learned in Al-Anon to help me through this ongoing loss, even though the situation has nothing to do with alcohol. The First Step says, "We admitted we were powerless over alcohol." We are also powerless over other diseases like Alzheimer's. What I do have power over are my own actions. I have the power to be patient, nonjudgmental, and supportive. When I forget this, I can focus on the slogans.

"Easy Does It" reminds me that my partner's mother is coping the best she can, and so is everyone around her. If someone says or does something out of stress, I need not react inappropriately. When she arranged her undergarments as an art show in the bathroom, I was surprised to find myself thinking, "How Important Is It?" Appearances might just be less important than enjoying the time we have left with her.

With Alzheimer's, as with alcoholism, there are good days and bad days. "One Day at a Time" reminds me that I don't have to get through the rest of this disease today. I just need to deal with today's symptoms today. Tomorrow may be different. If not, it will be another day and I can deal with whatever happens then.

As my partner's mother continues to deteriorate, I am sure the tools of the program will help me through. And perhaps I'll be able to share these tools with others. What a relief to know that I can use the Al-Anon program in other areas of my life besides alcoholism.

When the disease of alcoholism hit our family, I didn't have a name for it. I only knew that things were changing quickly, and for the worse. In looking back, I realize this was when I started to grieve. Since I've been in Al-Anon, I have experienced many changes—most recently, in my relationship with my daughter. I received a note from her that read, "Don't contact me, Dad." If such a note had arrived 10 years ago, I would have immediately contacted my daughter to ask her what was wrong; but today I am no longer the peacemaker or the rescuer.

I don't know what has prompted this action on my daughter's part, but I do know that I have no control over her choices. All I can do is ask my Higher Power to help us both through this period. I'm uncertain what I will do if my daughter makes contact with me in the future. My Higher Power reminds me from time to time that the choice is mine whether to approach a situation from a place of fear or love, but that choice is for the future. For today, it helps to talk with my Sponsor and share at meetings. Daily reading of Al-Anon literature also helps. Thank goodness I no longer have to grieve alone as I did in the past.

The loss of my relationships with my mother-in-law and sister have been especially challenging for me. At first, I felt shock and anger that they refused to accept my commitment to recovery. Guilt quickly followed, convincing me I was a terrible person because my recovery made them uncomfortable. I believe they want a relationship with me as much as I want one with them, but we differ in the kind of relationship we want. Today I understand that I don't need to force my recovery on them. My responsibility is to make amends when possible without harming others. Instead of defending my decisions, I've learned to say, "I'm sorry if you feel hurt or rejected by my recovery. That is not my intention."

I no longer want to have relationships that are based on enabling and unhealthy behavior. Today I can accept that my mother-in-law and my sister choose not to be in a relationship with me, and still leave the door open to the possibility of a limited relationship with them in the future. I grieve the loss of my relationship with these two people I love. I can remember the good qualities I know are still there in them, though they are often hidden by the disease of alcoholism. I can still love them even if I am not in contact with them.

Some years ago, a man I sponsored decided he no longer wanted me as a Sponsor. He told me his girlfriend suspected I was gay and she feared I would convert him. He didn't want to jeopardize their relationship, so he therefore decided he could no longer spend time with me. At that point, I was able to let him know that I was indeed gay, and the only reason I hadn't told him earlier was that it was a recent realization I was still learning to accept. I also reassured him that I would not have agreed to be his Sponsor if I had been romantically interested in him.

We parted ways, but his rejection gnawed at me. I felt hurt and continued to dwell on the incident for some time. True to the family disease of alcoholism, although presented with numerous examples of others who valued my friendship, I remained focused on the one person who didn't.

Eventually I shared my feelings with an Al-Anon friend, saying, "I just don't understand it. If he really practiced the Al-Anon program, he would put the focus on himself. It shouldn't matter what anyone else is, does, or says, because it's not a reflection on him." My friend smiled and replied, "Well, then, I guess you have your answer." It took a while for her message to sink in, but she had taken my pointed finger and aimed it back at me. The answer to dealing with this loss was to focus on myself. It was important for me to take my own inventory, to do what I needed for myself, and to "Live and Let Live." Other people's opinions and decisions are none of my business, and I need not take them personally. While my loss was real and I had every reason to grieve, my remaining friendships were just as real. Where I put my attention was my choice.

I was already a member of Al-Anon at the time of my divorce. When it came to marriage, I had a closed mind. I believed people should stay together. When mine ended, I thought I would die.

The loss of my daughter's presence at family gatherings was almost more than I could bear. I didn't want to share her on holidays with a co-parent in another city. I wanted her all to myself. When she moved away at age 15, I thought I would never survive the sorrow, shame, and loneliness. My extended family of in-laws was lost to me as well, and though I never dreamed that my closest friends would stop calling after my divorce, they did. I resented that I no longer fit in with the married couples my husband and I once knew. It seemed everything I cared about had run away from me, and I saw myself as a failure for failing those I loved.

I kept going to meetings and began to learn a new way of life in Al-Anon. I began to find my lost family through the new and loving friendships I made with other Al-Anon members. Little by little, I began to feel alive again, to feel more confident and worthy of love. My former narrow world began to get wider as I learned new things and met new people. As my life became fuller, I almost forgot how much I had once hurt. Then my daughter moved back home for her last year of high school—a new beginning together.

I have found a sense of renewed purpose through service. My experience allows me to offer compassion and encouragement to others who are going through similar losses. Al-Anon has provided me with precious spiritual gifts that led me to find wholeness and healing from my divorce. Today I can say I am free from the grief that once consumed me.

Questions for reflection and meditation

- What relationship am I grieving today?
- Have I made a "searching and fearless moral inventory" to explore my role in the alcoholic relationship?
- As I recover, how are my expectations of family and friends changing?
- If I am currently struggling with whether or not to leave a relationship, what issues are affecting my decision?
- Do I grieve differently if the loss of a relationship is involuntary or due to my choice?

Death of a Loved One

*"The disease of alcoholism leaves
mourners in its wake."*

There is perhaps no greater loss, and certainly none more permanent, than the death of a loved one. Many of us have been shocked to receive the news of our loved one's sudden death, while others may have been watching slow deterioration over the years. The death of a loved one leaves a lasting imprint on our hearts, whether we have lost a spouse or partner, child, family member, pet, friend, or Sponsor.

Though the process of grieving is similar in any loss, our grief can be different depending on the relationship. It feels different to lose a child instead of a spouse, or to lose a parent rather than a sibling. Many of us affected by the disease of alcoholism often have closer relationships with friends than we do with family. For us, the death of a friend can be more devastating than the death of a family member.

A death due to alcoholism can also feel different from other deaths we may have experienced. When our loved one dies without sobriety, lost too is any hope that the alcoholic would find help. We grieve for the relationship we yearned for with our loved one and for the many ways alcoholism has affected our lives. We might feel as if we have a whole lifetime of losses to mourn. The truth is, we have been grieving long before our loved one's death.

Understanding our feelings

As long as the alcoholic was still living, we held out hope for the possibility of recovery. We may have believed that if we prayed hard enough, we could have prevented the alcoholic's death. Now we may feel like our prayers have gone unanswered. If our loved one never found sobriety, we may feel anger over their inability to admit they had a problem and find help. We may be angry at the devastating ways alcoholism has affected our lives, or at the disease itself and the insidious way it destroys families and ruins lives.

So much of our early recovery is about the journey from denial to acceptance. Once we realize how denial has affected our lives, we don't ever want to go back there. But when we first hear the news of our loved one's death, it may be too much to accept at once. Our first reaction may be to feel numb. This can be especially confusing for those of us who have worked so hard to face our feelings.

Without denial, however, we may not be able to function at all. We would most likely not be able to make the necessary funeral or burial arrangements, take care of the many logistical details that need tending to when someone dies, or be there for our children or other family members. We probably wouldn't be able to get out of bed without a little bit of denial at work in us. When dealing with a death, denial helps protect us until we are ready to accept what has happened. Though feeling numb can be disconcerting, we can trust that it is temporary.

Relief

When her husband died, one member was surprised to feel a profound sense of relief: "It meant I would be free—freer than I'd ever been in our life together." One man was relieved to know that his wife was no longer suffering in the grips of the disease. A parent shared, "I'm not sure my son would have found peace on this earth. But I'm grateful he didn't leave behind a wife or child who would have to go through the pain of his alcoholism." Many of us are surprised to feel relief when the alcoholic dies.

Such feelings of relief can often lead us to question whether something is wrong with us. If we feel relief, we wonder, does it mean that we are glad the alcoholic is gone? Those who don't understand the disease of alcoholism may criticize or misjudge us, assuming our feelings of relief mean we didn't love the alcoholic. For fear of being perceived as callous, we might hesitate in admitting our feelings of relief, even to other Al-Anon members. We may worry that our feelings are unique, and that no one will be able to understand us.

If we take the risk to share about what we're feeling with our Sponsor or another Al-Anon member, we may find that we're not the only ones to have experienced these emotions. Our feelings of relief don't mean we didn't love the alcoholic. Perhaps our relief is a sign of our compassion for one who is no longer suffering. Perhaps we're relieved that we ourselves have been set free.

Facing a suicide or sudden death

Suicide is one of the tragic realities of alcoholism that, sadly, many of us have had to face. The pain of living with an addiction can become too much for some to bear. For those who follow this path, the decision to take their own lives may have felt like the only way out of their suffering. Receiving the news of a suicide can turn our world upside down. After the initial shock, we may blame ourselves for not seeing the warning signs. We may feel somehow responsible, believing we could have done something to prevent it.

Likewise many alcoholics die suddenly and unexpectedly from ignored or unforeseen health problems or alcohol-related accidents. Though we may never be entirely prepared for the reality of any death, facing a suicide or sudden death carries its own particular weight. We are robbed of the chance to say goodbye to our loved one, to deal with any unfinished business that may have been lingering between us, or to make amends.

We may vacillate between blaming the alcoholic and ourselves. We can't help but feel as if our loved one's death could have been avoided. If only we had tried harder, we tell ourselves, maybe we could have prevented this. If only I had pushed more. If only I hadn't pushed so much. If only the alcoholic wasn't so stubborn. If only.

The "if onlys" are a natural reaction to the news that our loved one is truly gone. It's part of how reality sinks in as our minds cope with shock. Though we may try to analyze or make sense of our loved one's death, the truth is, we may or may not ever fully understand.

Taking the First Step helps us recognize that we cannot control anyone else's life. Telling ourselves we are to blame for another person's death puts a tremendous burden upon us. In admitting our powerlessness over the actions of our loved ones, we begin to see that their lives were out of our control. Only when we can accept this, can we truly begin to accept their death. When her fiancé took his own life, one member came to realize, "Even if I saw the signs and could have postponed the act for a day, week, or month, it was never really in my power to control or change the outcome."

In facing a suicide or sudden death, we may feel as if our Higher Power has given us more than we can handle. In our frustration, we may shut out our Higher Power for a while. If we are unable to pray for ourselves, we can ask others to pray for us. It's okay to be angry. It's okay to take time out. Our Higher Power can handle it. Just as with any relationship, we will go through periods of anger. Why should our relationship with our Higher Power be any different? We aren't doing any of our relationships any favors when we deny our feelings. In fact, being comfortable enough to express ourselves shows the strength and resilience of the relationship— even with our Higher Power.

Unresolved issues and unfinished business

We may continue to be affected by the disease of alcoholism even after the alcoholic has died. If we were fortunate, we were able to resolve any problems in our relationship before our loved one's death. Some of us, however, didn't have that opportunity and are now left with unfinished business. If we haven't had the chance to voice or resolve our grievances or to make amends, we may feel weighed down with guilt, regret, or resentment.

We can still work on our relationship even though our loved one has died. In fact, some members have acknowledged that the alcoholic's death freed them to openly examine some of the issues they were unable to address or resolve while their loved one was still living. If our loved one has just recently died, the thought of delving into our unfinished business may feel daunting right now. Any outstanding issues we may have had in our relationships will still be there tomorrow, next month, next year, or until we are ready and able to deal with them.

We don't have to tackle every problem or issue at once. One member's journey through the Steps led him to the following insight: "I finally learned I couldn't undo all my defects of character in a few weeks or months." Our slogans "First Things First" and "One Day at a Time" can help take some of the weight off our shoulders. We can allow ourselves to take a few deep breaths and deal with what requires our attention at the moment. It is probably enough right now that we are dealing with our loved one's death. When we are ready, we can begin the process of examining any outstanding issues in our relationship. Taking a Fourth Step inventory and sharing it with our Sponsor or a trusted friend can help us see how we might have contributed to any difficulties in our relationship. Yet we need only accept responsibility for our own actions. When someone dies, we can easily glorify their good qualities and temporarily forget their faults. We can remind ourselves that whatever issues existed had to do with both people and were not solely our responsibility.

Though our loved one is no longer with us physically, we can still make amends if we need to. We might consider writing our thoughts in a letter. We could take the letter to our loved one's gravesite or to another quiet space and read it either silently or aloud. Or we could share the letter with our Sponsor. We can do whatever feels right for us. The important thing is to find some way to articulate our thoughts and feelings.

Coping with the death of a Sponsor

In the course of our recovery, some of us will face the death of our Sponsor. For many of us, our Sponsor was the first person to love us unconditionally, to know our deepest secrets, our struggles, and our successes. Our Sponsor supported, challenged, and encouraged us—believing in us even when we didn't believe in ourselves. Some of us have felt closer to our Sponsor than we did to our own families. The loss of someone who has been such an integral part of our recovery can be devastating.

We may panic at the thought of no longer having a Sponsor, and the prospect of finding a new one can be daunting. We can trust that someday we will find a new Sponsor, but we don't have to pressure ourselves to do so before we are ready. We can trust that our Higher Power will lead us to someone new when the time is right. Until then, we might spend some time in meditation, reflecting on how our Sponsor helped us get where we are today. Another way we can let the wisdom of our Sponsor live on is through our own gift of service, in whatever form we choose. In this way, we can pass along the love that was given to us so freely by our Sponsor.

Fear of never getting over it

Grief is not an orderly process. It is not logical, has no rules, and disrupts our lives. While in the throes of grief, we may have a hard time imagining that we could feel any differently than we do at this moment. We may fear that the intensity of our emotions will never diminish, and that if we start crying, we'll never stop. At the same time, we might feel a certain devotion to our sadness, believing it to be a demonstration of our love. Based on this belief, we may struggle with allowing ourselves to feel happy.

There are some losses we will never get over. Our relationship to them will most likely change over time, but they will always be with us. We can trust that the Al-Anon principles are still at work in us, even if we don't feel we have the strength to practice them. It can help to remind ourselves that just as our recovery is a process, so too is our grief. We don't have to do it perfectly, nor do we have to handle all our feelings perfectly. While others may be questioning why we're not over our loss, in Al-Anon we are free to grieve in our own way and at our own pace.

The safe haven of our fellowship gives us the courage to face our feelings and to express our grief as we are ready. When we allow ourselves to be vulnerable, we take an important step toward easing our pain. Likewise, when we take the risk to open up, we give hope to others who might be struggling with their own unspoken grief. The simple yet courageous act of sharing our story can help others in ways we may never know.

Permission to move forward

"My friends in Al-Anon let me be exactly who I am and where I am," one man said. "At the same time, they gently encourage me not to stay there longer than necessary." We may be hesitant to allow ourselves to move forward, or we may feel as though we are betraying our loved one by going on with our lives.

How do we give ourselves permission to move forward? We can take the lessons we have learned from our grief and, as Step Twelve suggests, apply them in all our affairs. We can keep the memory of our loved one alive through our service in Al-Anon. We can do something each day to take care of ourselves physically, emotionally, and spiritually. Before a meeting begins, we can pray that we be open to hearing something that will comfort us. The love we receive in Al-Anon can also help us move forward.

"The constant reminder that I am loved in Al-Anon helps me remember that the one I lost is not my only source of love."

Our lives will never be the same after our loved one's death, nor should they be. Moving forward does not mean we forget about our loved one or that we have finished grieving. Though moving on may seem unlikely for us, we have seen it happen for others. Fortunately our Higher Power's plan for us does not depend entirely on our agreement to it. Even if we are unable to believe in a future for ourselves, we can trust that it will still be given to us.

> *"I still miss my husband. I always will. But thanks to Al-Anon, I am able to let the past go, live today to its fullest, and look forward to whatever my Higher Power has in mind for me tomorrow."*

Members share experience, strength, and hope: Death of a loved one

My life changed forever when I attended my first Al-Anon beginners meeting at the gentle urging of a kind friend. My son had made a serious suicide attempt, and I was in a sea of pain and terror. In Al-Anon I found care, understanding, support, and a wealth of information about a new way of life. For the next year, I learned to accept the realities of addiction and gained compassion for my tormented alcoholic and drug addicted son. I mourned the loss of my hopes and dreams for my child. Gradually I came to accept my inability to save my son. In the infancy of my newfound spirituality, I imagined wrapping my son in a quilt and placing him in God's arms.

My son lost his battle with alcohol and drugs and committed suicide a year after I began the program. I was swept up in such a whirlwind of pain and devastation, even breathing took concerted effort. Assailed by guilt, I questioned every aspect of my motherhood. How could I have let him down so badly? Why didn't I do more to save him? I didn't leave Al-Anon altogether, but I was no longer sure what was there for me. It seemed that everyone else's child was in recovery, and somehow I had failed. I went to meetings occasionally but was usually unable to speak. I just sat there. I loved to get the hugs and caring, but generally I felt like an alien. Eventually I stopped attending meetings altogether.

By the grace of God, I stayed in touch with some Al-Anon friends, and after a few months, I was able to return. I know now that my Higher Power was guiding me back, and I soon found a Sponsor. I embraced the first three Steps and accepted I was powerless over this disease. I realized the only possibility for me was to turn my intolerable grief over to God.

I have learned so much about surviving loss and am grateful to have found other souls with whom I can grieve and share my pain. Without Al-Anon, I don't believe I could have survived the loss of my son.

After 11 years of sobriety, my husband chose to take his own life. The numbness and grief that followed were overwhelming. I felt a deep sense of loss on so many levels. I also felt tremendous anger—anger that he would do this to me and our family, and anger that he could not find another solution. Most of all, I was angry that his departure took all our shared history along with it. We had been elementary school classmates and high school sweethearts. Through 35 years of marriage, we had somehow always been able to work things out. Now everything I had shared with him was gone.

I returned to my home group immediately. People there were compassionate and caring. Through meetings and working with my Sponsor, I came to realize that my husband's death was his choice and that I was not responsible for another's choices. I truly learned the meaning of "to accept the things I cannot change" from the Serenity Prayer. Working my program allows me to detach from someone else's choices and gives me the freedom to make my own.

When I first came to Al-Anon, my son was an active alcoholic and addict, my husband was in the midst of a major clinical depression, and I was at my wit's end. In Al-Anon I found others who had similar experiences, yet I listened only selectively to their stories. I was going to meetings but not working the program. I still clung to the hope that if I went into recovery, my loved ones would follow. Then one day, I suddenly realized that while everyone else was talking about taking care of themselves and focusing on their own behavior, I was continuing to talk about my son, my husband—everyone but me! That realization marked the beginning of my recovery.

Several years later, my worst fears came true. My son died of an accidental overdose at the age of 24. Less than two months later, his distraught father took his own life. I went into a state of shock and grief that overwhelmed me. I had always believed I could survive almost anything—but never the loss of my family.

Today I find that I am not only surviving, but I am grateful to be alive. The Al-Anon program has made all the difference. During my darkest hours, I tortured myself with the question of what I might have done that could have made a difference. I remember spending many nights in the grip of the worst kind of fear and hopelessness. At these times, I focused on the Eleventh Step, asking God to show me the path and give me the strength to walk it. I would pray, "Your path, God, not mine." And by what seemed like a miracle, a path would open before me to get me through the night, the next hour, or sometimes only the next minute. Once I surrendered my will, I saw that my Higher Power was there—holding me through the crisis.

Growing up in an alcoholic home, one of the few consistent and reliable things in my life was my beloved cat. She was always happy to see me and grateful for even the smallest acts of love.

Whenever I was sad, afraid, hurt, or lonely, she would listen to me without judgment. I would hold her and cry, and she would gaze up at me and purr as if to say, "This too shall pass." She provided me with comfort and companionship during some of the most tumultuous times of my life.

She lived into her late teen years and well into my Al-Anon recovery years. Because I had known the unconditional love of my pet, I was able to look for the same qualities in my new Al-Anon friends. Al-Anon gave me the love, acceptance, and guidance I so desperately needed. When my cat began to decline, my Al-Anon friends helped me prepare to let her go. The night she died, I knew exactly what I needed to do and had the courage to do it. I held her in my arms and thanked her for her love and friendship. She gazed at me with her near sightless eyes and told me she was ready to go. She passed away peacefully purring, no longer in pain.

My Al-Anon family recognized that love takes many forms, including the special relationship between a child from an alcoholic home and her pet. They let me talk about my loss without ever minimizing my grief, and never mocking the impact she had on my life. Today I know that grief is the price I pay for having loved and having been loved well.

I struggled for years trying to save a 25-year marriage that just wasn't working. The program helped me realize that I could no longer wait for my husband to get sober so I could get on with my life. If I was to have any life at all, I would have to make a decision. Moreover, I began to see the effects my husband's drinking and violence were having on our children. I could no longer stand by and allow them to be damaged by his unacceptable behavior. If he chose to continue to drink, I didn't have to go insane or die with him. My husband was shocked when I filed for divorce. After so many years of empty threats, he never believed I would actually follow through.

The day our divorce was final, I grieved for the end of a dream and a marriage that could have been. I grieved for the husband he used to be and for the loving father he could have been. I grieved for the wasted years of worrying and trying to control his drinking.

Two years ago, my husband passed away from the disease of alcoholism. By that time, we had been divorced for many years, and I had learned acceptance. Because of the program, all five of our children were able to have understanding and forgiveness for their father. At the funeral, I mourned for a talented, gifted, loving person who was trapped in a disease he couldn't free himself from. At the same time, I was able to feel empathy, forgiveness, and relief that he was finally out of his misery.

I have been able to find happiness again. Today I know that no matter what grief I may have to face in my life, my Higher Power and the program will be there to help me through it.

When a newcomer asked me to be her Sponsor, I felt humbled. While she went through a painful divorce and faced the challenges of single parenthood, I listened and offered comfort. I was unaware of my sponsee's psychological issues until I learned she had attempted to take her own life. She was admitted to the hospital and began treatment. I knew she needed help from professionals, and I encouraged her to remain in treatment.

It became evident to me that I could no longer give her the help she needed to overcome her problems. I knew I would have to ask her to find another Sponsor, but it never seemed like a good time to tell her.

Three months later, I returned from an out of town trip to find a message from her on my answering machine. I made arrangements with my own Sponsor to discuss the dilemma and find some clarity about the situation. That night I received a phone call that my sponsee had committed suicide. I was devastated.

For the next few years, I was deeply depressed. I could not under-stand why she killed herself. Did I forget to tell her that tomorrow would be a better day? Did I fail her as a Sponsor? Could I have prevented her death if I was home and could have spoken with her? How could I have considered leaving her as a Sponsor? Why did this have to happen to her children, parents, siblings, friends, and me? I began to avoid Al-Anon members who wanted me to sponsor them, and eventually I withdrew from the program.

During that time, I discovered that being alone in my grief was preventing me from healing from my loss. I eventually returned to Al-Anon and began sharing my pain. With the unconditional love of other members, I came to realize I did all I could to help my sponsee. Today I find comfort knowing she is with a God of her understanding.

I came to Al-Anon because of the alcoholic in my life, but when we eventually divorced, I often asked myself why I continued to go to Al-Anon. After all, I was no longer living with an alcoholic. Today I realize I keep coming back so I can "practice these prin-ciples in all my affairs."

With the help of Al-Anon and my Higher Power, I was able to heal from the pain of losing my marriage. Several years after the divorce, having had little to no contact with the alcoholic, I received that dreaded phone call that he had died from the disease. I had hoped and prayed many times that he would walk through the doors of Alcoholics Anonymous and get sober. That never happened.

With many years of Al-Anon behind me, I had come to accept the disease and feel compassion for my ex-husband. Now that he was dead, I knew he was no longer suffering from the disease. Reading the *Just for Today* bookmark was very comforting. It allowed me to reflect on the good and the bad in our relationship, and to make amends for the ways I had behaved and reacted to living with active alcoholism. I now realize I did the best I could at the time.

I was allowed to participate in the planning of my ex-husband's services, and I asked that *Just for Today* be read. Today I am grateful for having loved an alcoholic and for having been brought to the rooms of Al-Anon.

We often refer to alcoholism as the elephant in the living room, but the hippopotamus in the living room is death. For many of us, our greatest fear is that the alcoholic will die, yet we don't seem to talk about it enough. I found my 31-year-old son dead this past summer. He had just returned from a 28-day stay in a rehabilitation program—his fifth such stay. He had been abusing alcohol and drugs for more than half his life. I believe his death came very quickly and that I couldn't have prevented it. It was ruled an accidental overdose.

I'm not sure I could have gotten through that day and the days that followed if it weren't for Al-Anon. After calling the police, I sat outside and repeated the Serenity Prayer over and over. By the time the police arrived, I was able to talk to them calmly, then call my husband. It was hot that day. When a neighbor asked if there was something she could do, I asked for water. I was able to choose a funeral home and decide on cremation without hesitating. With so many close calls over the years, I had given much thought to what we might need to do if our son died.

There was so much to tend to after my son's death, but I was able to take care of myself by doing a little bit each day. I was helped by a story in *One Day at a Time in Al-Anon* about a woman whose husband had died. To deal with her grief, she thought about what she would be doing if this horrible thing hadn't happened, and then she did it. That helped me get through this crisis.

In many ways, dealing with my son's life was more difficult than dealing with his death. A few years ago, he had managed a year of sobriety. I will always be grateful for the opportunity we had to see him hold a job, pay his bills, take care of his health, and participate in family gatherings. When he relapsed, I was able to really accept my son as he was—someone who might be sober at times, and actively drinking at others. I attended Al-Anon meetings through it all, and continue to do so. Al-Anon once gave me hope for a better future for my son. It now sustains me through my loss.

Questions for reflection and meditation

- What type of relationship did I have with the person whose death I am grieving today?
- Do I blame myself for any part of my loved one's death?
- Have I given myself permission to acknowledge all my feelings about the death of my loved one?
- What tradition or symbolic ritual might help me resolve any unfinished business or make amends, if necessary?
- What role does my Higher Power play at this moment in my life?
- How does this loss affect my attitude about the future?

Dealing with Our Feelings

"I needed to feel to heal."

Healing from our losses depends so much upon our willingness to feel. This can be challenging for all of us, but especially so for those of us who were raised to believe that certain feelings were "bad" or "wrong." We may have adapted ourselves to such beliefs by learning to bury any painful emotions. Living with the disease of alcoholism often led us to further disregard our feelings.

Discounting our feelings may have once been a necessary survival skill, but that way of life no longer works for us. In Al-Anon we learn that we have a right to our feelings. Part of treating ourselves well means learning to accept *all* our feelings without judging them. As one member came to realize about his grief: "What I needed was not to counter or correct it, but to endure and honor it." When it comes to our emotions, chances are we won't always like how we feel. In Al-Anon we are able to express our feelings without being judged.

> *"At my first Al-Anon meeting, I remember crying for the first time ever in the presence of strangers. Instead of responding with discomfort or judgment, they offered me their phone numbers and told me they loved me. For someone who'd always been told that tears were ugly, this was a true miracle."*

While we are grieving, we might wish we didn't have to feel certain painful emotions, but the fact that we are feeling them means we are better prepared to face them than we once were. As we grow in Al-Anon, we find that we are able to feel our feelings as they happen instead of months or years later. We come to realize that our true strength lies not in minimizing or denying our feelings, but in our willingness to feel and express all our emotions.

Permission to feel

As children we may have been told, "Nice girls don't get angry," or "Boys don't cry." As a result, we may have learned to hide our feelings, only allowing ourselves the freedom to feel when we were alone. For those of us who were not allowed to express certain emotions, giving ourselves permission to do so today is momentous.

"My family drank and socialized at my father's funeral. I was told I was an embarrassment because I was crying."

One of the effects of living with alcoholism is that it's often not safe to talk about our feelings, much less express them. In Al-Anon we learn that whatever we are feeling is okay, and that emotions are neither good nor bad.

Some of us spent so much of our lives aware of the feelings of those around us that we may have a difficult time recognizing our own. While our sensitivity to others may have helped us become more compassionate human beings, it may also have led us to internalize other people's emotions. As a result, we may feel confusion over which feelings belong to us and which belong to someone else.

"The Serenity Prayer helps me accept my sometimes slow pace in identifying my feelings. It has helped me learn patience, recognizing that this is merely one aspect of who I am."

Identifying our feelings does not come easily for everyone. Some may require more time than others to get clear about what we're feeling. Even if we do know what we're feeling, we may be confused by the conflicting emotions we experience in grief. We may be sad one moment and angry the next. It's okay to give ourselves time and space to gain clarity about our feelings. For some, writing in a journal helps us better understand what we're feeling. Others have found that time spent in prayer or meditation can open our hearts to buried emotions. Listening to others talk about their feelings can also help us get in touch with our own.

Awareness of painful feelings can leave us anxious or afraid. Our fear of grieving can be so powerful at times it might seem safer to stuff our feelings than to feel them. Some of us have an easier time talking about feelings than actually feeling them. For instance, we might rationalize our anger by justifying the wrongs done to us, when what we may truly be feeling beneath our anger is pain and sadness. Intellectualizing our emotions can keep us from feeling our pain at its deepest level. Some of us may have excessively used drugs, alcohol, food, sex, exercise, cleaning, shopping, or other compulsive behaviors in an attempt to escape our feelings. Or perhaps we obsessed about other people's problems as a way to avoid our own.

"If I stuff my feelings, they never go away."

Avoiding or minimizing our feelings can eventually become an automatic response—almost like a reflex. For a while, our avoidance may have kept our pain at a distance, but avoiding our feelings long-term usually leads to more problems. We may have thought we were keeping our feelings at bay, but the more we resisted them, the more power they gained over us.

As with any new behavior, we might struggle at first with finding a balance between minimizing our feelings and focusing too much on them. If we've spent the majority of our lives closed off from our feelings, we might tend to go to extremes at first.

"I do indeed make mountains out of molehills, but I believe
that's because I once skimmed over catastrophic events."

To make up for those times when we looked the other way, we might tend to examine every incident as if it were under a microscope. Analyzing every feeling in this way can leave us exhausted. We can trust that, in time, we'll learn to distinguish between those feelings we can let go of and those that require our full attention. When we're feeling overwhelmed, we can take a moment to slow down our thoughts and bring ourselves back to the present. If we start to panic, we can remind ourselves that in this moment we are safe, even if what we are feeling may scare us.

The more time we spend around recovering people who take the risk to be open and honest about their feelings, the safer we feel about expressing our own. In time we come to understand that whatever we are feeling is worthy of our attention. We don't have to suffer in silence with our grief.

Coping with a multitude of feelings

At times we may find ourselves wishing we could escape the intensity of our emotions. We may have moments in our grief where we try to convince ourselves that life was easier before recovery, when we either denied or minimized what was happening to us. Now that we have opened our hearts to experience our feelings, we realize that we can't remain the same. This is both one of the gifts and hardships of feeling with an open heart.

Before we came to Al-Anon, many of us had no idea how to deal with our grief. We may have played the minimizing game, trying to convince ourselves or others that things were not that bad, that we were fine, or that we were strong and could handle any storm that came our way. Some of us were conditioned to see any display of emotion as a sign of weakness or lack of control. Even if we have been recovering for a long time, we may still struggle with accepting certain feelings.

In Al-Anon we learn to value all our feelings, even the ones that make us uncomfortable. Our Steps give us the tools to recognize and share our feelings, to love and nurture ourselves, and to trust that whatever we are feeling will eventually pass. We will have good days and bad days. Some days we will be able to talk about our grief. Other days our sorrow will be indescribable. Some days we won't want to get out of bed. While we are grieving, it's unrealistic to expect ourselves to function in the same ways we always have. It may take much longer to accomplish simple tasks, and we may be unable to concentrate on anything for longer than a few minutes. Some days the only thing we can do about our grief is turn it over to our Higher Power.

Numbness and denial

"By the time I got to Al-Anon I was numb. I'd been told I
needed to grieve, but I didn't know how, and I wasn't
willing to find out."

Our impulse to protect ourselves from the pain of grief can seem natural enough at first. However, when we keep ourselves from feeling anything at all, our lives can quickly become unmanageable.

Denial is one way we shield ourselves from reality, often because that reality is too much for us to bear. In this way, denial can help us through painful situations, allowing us time and space to become acclimated to the truth. Although denial can protect us from our pain, it can also hurt us. Remaining in a state of denial for too long can cause us to lose touch with ourselves. Pretending we are "fine" does little to improve the way we feel. Over time we can become so removed from what we are feeling, we don't even recognize when we are hurting. Just as Step One helped us admit our powerlessness over the disease of alcoholism, it can also help when it comes to accepting our powerlessness over our feelings.

In Al-Anon we learn that we cannot escape our feelings; we only postpone them. Since we can never entirely hide from our feelings, we may find our grief coming out in unexpected ways. Some of us become anxious and depressed. One member said she became filled with anxiety whenever she lost or misplaced something, unable to calm down until she found it. Others try to stay busy to avoid having to feel. Without our realizing it, our efforts at trying to control our pain can soon become a way of life.

"If I mistakenly stop long enough to feel what's inside me, all
I feel is pain and loss. No wonder I don't want to feel my
feelings! Someone recently suggested I rent some sad movies
so I could cry. I guess I should, but I'm too busy to cry."
"I've always been afraid that the intense feelings would swallow
me up and I'd get lost."

One of our fears may be that if we faced the reality of our loss, we'd lose ourselves. The thought of letting go of our denial can seem scary. We may be afraid of what we'll feel if we let down our guard. In Al-Anon we learn that facing our feelings doesn't mean we have to allow ourselves to get stuck in them. Steps Four and Five provide us with some structure as we peel away the layers and begin to face the painful feelings we have been running from. These Steps ask us to be vulnerable—to honestly examine our flaws and our fears.

In Step Four, we make "a searching and fearless moral inventory of ourselves." As we delve into our past, we begin to understand how we arrived where we are today. As we apply this Step, we gain self-awareness about how our denial may have served us. Some members have found it helpful to start by making a list of our fears. When we can name our fears, they begin to lose their power. We can ask ourselves what we fear might happen if we were to feel a particular emotion. Our Fourth Step inventory can help us gain important insights we might not otherwise see. We examine our personal history, the messages we received in the past, and our part in how we've allowed those messages to control us in the present. The purpose of this Step is not to blame ourselves or cause shame, but to look at ourselves with compassion and understanding.

Step Five asks us to admit to ourselves, our Higher Power, and another human being "the exact nature of our wrongs." Self-awareness is important, but this Step suggests we include others in the process too. When we turn to our Higher Power and another human being, we admit we need help and cannot recover alone. Some of us will take the Fifth Step with our Sponsor, while others will choose a clergy member or spiritual advisor, a therapist, or a trusted friend. What's most important is that we choose someone trustworthy and compassionate—someone with whom we feel safe enough to be open and honest. When we admit how we've damaged ourselves or others by hiding from our feelings, we can begin to heal.

Guilt and regret

Many of us who have lived with alcoholism became experts at blaming ourselves. The alcoholics in our lives may have blamed us for their drinking, or we may have told ourselves it was our fault. Guilt, whether self-imposed or put upon us by others, can trap us in a downward spiral. We can easily get stuck in the "if onlys," telling ourselves our lives would have been better if only we had done things differently. We may have convinced ourselves that if only we had tried harder, we could have prevented the alcoholic's problems, illness, or death.

> *"Thanks to Al-Anon, I no longer believe that my thoughts, feelings, or God make bad things happen. Sometimes bad things happen and it's no one's fault."*

We may indeed wish certain details of our lives were different, but that doesn't mean we have the power to change them. Al-Anon helps us see that we only have the power to change ourselves, our behaviors, and our reactions. Sometimes our actions do affect the course of certain events, and for those we can hold ourselves accountable. But we're not responsible for everything. Even if we were the worst spouse, parent, child, or friend in the world, we would not be responsible for the actions of others. When we assume responsibility for other people's behaviors, we prevent them from taking responsibility for themselves.

If we didn't have the opportunity to reconcile with the alcoholic, we might feel guilty for things left unsaid. Others feel guilty for wishing the alcoholic would die. We might regret not feeling as badly as expected when the alcoholic gets sick or dies. Just because we don't feel sad today over our loss doesn't mean we never will, and it doesn't mean we aren't still grieving. We can remind ourselves that feelings aren't facts. Just because we felt or thought something doesn't mean we caused it to happen. If we had that kind of power, we would have gotten the alcoholic sober long ago!

Though we often use the terms "regret" and "guilt" interchangeably, they really mean different things. Regret is wishing that something could have turned out differently. Regrets can wreak emotional havoc and keep us focused on "what could have been." Many of us carry regrets for the ways we reacted to the alcoholism in our lives—whether in our marriages, partnerships, parenting, or friendships. We may wish we had done things differently, even though we may not have known how to at the time. We may feel the need to make amends for certain regrets, especially if our inaction may have caused harm to others.

Guilt, on the other hand, is a feeling of remorse for having knowingly done something wrong. Guilt is that nagging feeling we get when we know we have hurt someone. Sometimes the hurts we inflict are like surface wounds, and sometimes they go deeper. If left unaddressed for too long, our guilt over certain events can consume us. If we're feeling guilt or regret over any of our past mistakes, we can turn to the Steps to make amends.

Being human means we will make mistakes. Criticizing ourselves for making them doesn't improve the situation. When we hold ourselves to such high standards of perfection, we often find it difficult to accept our humanity. If we spent our lives blaming ourselves for everything that ever went wrong, we may find it challenging at first to distinguish between earned and unearned guilt. It can help to talk with our Sponsor about those aspects of our guilt that cause us confusion. Once we determine what mistakes we are responsible for, we can take Steps Eight and Nine.

In Step Eight, we make a list of those persons we have harmed and become willing to make amends. Many of us have done as much if not more harm to ourselves than we have to anyone else, so we also remember to include ourselves on our list. If we've been in the habit of putting ourselves last, it might be good practice to put our name first. Blaming ourselves for everything and believing that we have hurt everyone around us can be just as damaging to our relationships as convincing ourselves we've never done anything to hurt anyone. If we're used to seeing ourselves as victims, it might be difficult at first to admit that we have, in fact, harmed others. Our intent in Step Eight is to be as honest and forthcoming as we can—not so we'll feel bad about ourselves, but so we can begin to free ourselves from guilt.

Step Nine opens the door for us to heal ourselves and our relationships. This Step is about making *direct* amends *wherever* possible. It's about doing what we can to heal our relationships without causing further harm. Making direct amends means facing the people we have harmed if at all possible. Sometimes, however, it's not possible to make direct amends. Perhaps the people we have harmed have made it clear that they want no contact from us, or perhaps they are no longer living. This doesn't mean we can't make amends, however.

Making amends may not happen in the way we had envisioned or expected, but we don't have to beat ourselves up for not getting around to it before now. We were simply waiting until we were ready. If our loved one is no longer living, we can express whatever it is we would like to say in a letter and then burn or bury it. Or we might try talking to our deceased loved one or visiting their gravesite.

If we're unable to be in direct contact with the person we have harmed, we can keep them in the quiet of our hearts during prayer or meditation. We can also make amends through our changed attitudes. After all, what we've learned from the Eighth and Ninth Steps can benefit all our relationships—not just with the person we've harmed.

Anger

*"Whether I lost someone I enjoyed or despised, it was
    still a loss."*

Grief doesn't only manifest itself through tears and sadness. Even if we feel nothing but anger for a time, we can still be grieving. Though it's natural to feel anger while we are grieving, many of us are uncomfortable with this feeling. Just hearing the word "anger" can lead many of us to react—especially if we have been affected by another's uncontrollable rage or physical and emotional abuse. Or perhaps the topic makes us uncomfortable because we are struggling with our own anger. Anger can be an important part of our grief and our healing. If our tendency has been to avoid anger, we may be unaware of what it can teach us. We can learn to give ourselves permission to feel our anger instead of denying it or running from it.

*"After a while, my rage was the only indication to me that I
    was alive."*

Anger may be one of the most confusing feelings we will have to confront while we are grieving. We may have told ourselves if we were a good person, if we were working a good program, or if we were spiritual enough, we wouldn't feel angry. Feeling angry has nothing to do with any of these things. In fact, working a good program means accepting all our feelings—including anger. Whatever shame we may feel about our anger does little to negate it. We may do everything in our power to convince ourselves that we shouldn't feel angry, but discounting or discrediting our feelings won't make them disappear—it may only intensify them. It's possible to get stuck in any feeling, and anger is no exception. We don't have to let our anger control us, but it can if we don't allow ourselves to feel it.

If we didn't have healthy models for expressing anger, we may become frightened or anxious whenever we're around angry people. Our own feelings of anger may also intimidate us, which can lead us to either suppress our feelings, or to act out inappropriately. Daily life with a violent alcoholic parent led one member to struggle for years with what it meant to express anger in a healthy way.

> *"My alcoholic father was the only one allowed to express anger. For years, I believed anger, rage, and violence were inextricably linked. Any display of anger frightened me, causing me to reflexively tense up during arguments or conflicts. In Al-Anon I discovered that not everyone who lived with alcoholism lived with violence. It took me a long time to realize that my father's rage was a separate problem, made worse by alcohol. In time I learned that I didn't have to be afraid of anger, as long as it was expressed appropriately."*

When we talk about expressing anger, we're not talking about flying into a rage. We can learn how to face and express anger in safe and healthy ways, and we can reasonably expect the same from others. Though another person's anger might feel uncomfortable to us, it doesn't always mean we are in a dangerous situation. Allowing others to feel and express their anger in ways that don't hurt us can help us see that anger is not something we have to fear. If someone else's anger crosses a boundary and becomes aggressive or violent, we can remove ourselves from that person's presence to assure our safety.

What does expressing anger in a healthy way mean? First, it means being aware that we're angry. Second, it means understanding why we are angry. Sometimes our anger lets us know we've been hurt. In fact, we may not even realize we're hurting until we get angry. In Al-Anon we learn we no longer have to hide from our pain. If we've been hurt by someone else's words or actions, we can tell that person how we feel.

If we're in the midst of an argument that continues to escalate, we can take time out to calm ourselves. It might not be wise to get behind the wheel of a car when we're upset, but we can step outside to take a few deep breaths, take a walk around the block, repeat the Serenity Prayer, or reflect on a slogan. Some members find that talking things out with our Sponsor or another Al-Anon member can help dissipate the intensity of our feelings. Once we've calmed down, we can ask ourselves why we feel angry. Has someone hurt us? Are we overtired or stressed? Is there something we can do to take care of ourselves that would help us feel better?

Some of us may be carrying unresolved hurts that continue to fuel our anger. At times we may feel angry at ourselves or others. Some members are angry at the disease of alcoholism.

> *I was angry at my father for choosing a bottle instead of his family, angry at the family history that contributed to my son's alcoholism, and angry at being caught in the ugliness of this disease.*

Some days, we wake up feeling angry at the world, unsure of how we got here. We may also have days when we feel angry at our Higher Power. One member was troubled by the anger she felt after her daughter was killed in a car accident: "I was so angry at God I could barely stand it. I had worked so hard at building a loving relationship with God, and now I was afraid because I was angry at that same God. Then someone at a meeting told me that God understood my anger. Hearing this helped. In time my anger lessened and I began to heal." Though anger at our Higher Power may be disconcerting to us, it might turn out to be the vehicle for a more intimate relationship.

> *I shut God out. I could no longer pray or meditate. With the help of my Sponsor, Al-Anon friends, and some outside help, I discovered it's okay to be angry with God. Gradually I was able to let go of my anger. Today my relationship with my Higher Power is even stronger than it was before.*

Letting go of our anger doesn't mean we condone the ways we've been mistreated, and it doesn't mean we won't still feel pain about our losses. We may still have some work to do before we are ready to let go of our anger. In time many of us have found that the more we embrace what our anger can teach us, the less likely we will be to fear it.

Depression and isolation

When emotions go unexpressed, we can become depressed, irritable, and emotionally unavailable to our loved ones and to ourselves. When we are hurting, our first impulse may be to withdraw from others until we feel better. Some days depression and loneliness can weigh on us, and we may feel as though no one understands what we're going through. We may find it difficult to connect with our Higher Power or with close friends at this time. Some days the mere thought of having a conversation can exhaust us.

There's a difference between taking time for ourselves and isolating. Sometimes that difference may be subtle. If we isolate for too long, pondering and obsessing over our feelings instead of sharing them, we may end up suffering needlessly.

A longtime member shared, "I believed my time in the program would be enough for me to overcome my grief. Before I knew it, I put up walls. I didn't ask for help, and therefore I didn't get any." Sometimes, we can build walls without even knowing it. Fear of being judged can keep us from opening up at meetings or from attending them at all. This only heightens our sense of isolation. A meeting might be the last place we want to be when we feel depressed, yet time spent at a meeting can bring us comfort when we could use it most. If it seems like too much effort to get ourselves to a meeting, we can call a friend and ask for a ride. If we don't feel like being around people we know, we can try another meeting. If we don't have the energy to speak, we don't have to force ourselves. Sometimes we get all we need when we give ourselves permission just to listen.

Although depression is a natural part of grieving, if we find it becoming persistent, we may want to seek professional help. Though Al-Anon may not solve all our problems, it can allow us to see that it's okay to ask for help. We don't have to feel ashamed if we are depressed. Feeling depressed doesn't mean we're not grieving or that we've failed to practice our program. It just means we may need some extra support through this difficult and trying time.

Why me?

In the midst of isolation and depression, it's easy to get caught up in wondering, "Why me?" Perhaps we were raised with the belief that terrible things were destined for us, or that we are being punished by our Higher Power or the universe. Or perhaps we believed that other people's actions got in the way of our happiness. Over time we may have inadvertently allowed our painful past to influence our belief that nothing good can come our way. This way of thinking can become deeply ingrained in us, and before we know it, we've landed in the role of victim. There's little harm in feeling sorry for ourselves from time to time, but staying there too long can keep us from healing and moving forward.

"I spent my early years in recovery doing some sick thinking about how bad I had it living with an active alcoholic. I would seek out other Al-Anon members who still lived with the active disease, and dismiss the experiences of others whose lives were different from mine. I found it useful to keep myself in a victim stance because it meant I didn't have to take any action."

Some of us may have learned that playing the role of victim by showing the world how awful our lives were was the only way we could get the attention and love we deserved. This belief may have been reinforced by the fact that certain people gave us more attention when we were struggling. Many of us have come to realize that this is not the sort of attention we truly desire. We may not have received the love we wanted in the past, but this does not mean we are unlovable. In Al-Anon we learn that we don't have to be in constant pain to be worthy of attention and love. The healthier we become, the more we will begin to attract people who will love us for who we are, rather than for how we've suffered.

Though terrible things may have happened to us, in Al-Anon we learn that we are not victims. Unlearning our old beliefs is not easy, but it can be done. One member tried to overcome his victim role simply by observing his actions. He found it helpful to think of himself as an objective reporter, paying attention to how he spoke about his life. This allowed him to see how often he framed his experiences negatively. If we're struggling to let go of our victim mentality, perhaps a key to healing lies in the simple act of giving ourselves loving attention.

> *"Recovery taught me that other people's actions or inactions are not necessarily designed to affect me. Seeing myself as a victim was a convenient way to keep my focus on others. When I finally accepted responsibility for myself, I could then see that I was a victim only of myself."*

The other side of grief

It can be hard to imagine our lives on the other side of grief. In moving on, we may fear we'll be abandoning our loved one, our dreams, our past, or our pain. The idea of going on with our lives can leave us feeling uneasy and guilty. Refusing to allow ourselves to move on benefits no one, and ultimately damages ourselves and others. We can still say yes to life without forgetting our losses. Perhaps moving on isn't about abandoning anyone else. Perhaps it's really about choosing not to abandon ourselves.

Many of us would agree that feelings can't be managed easily. In our grief, we may find it especially difficult to remember that our feelings are temporary. Whatever we are feeling at this moment is not necessarily a predictor of how we will feel tomorrow or even an hour from now.

"I can't put closure on my feelings. Closure is something that
happens to a house, not to feelings."

"This too shall pass" has helped many of us cope with our feelings during times of grief. When panicked by a crisis or overwhelmed by sadness, it can serve as a helpful reminder that whatever we are feeling will eventually lessen. For others, this expression hits a nerve. Some have found it dismissive, as though we are being told to "get over it." If others are afraid of our pain, they may use this expression in an effort to ease their own discomfort. Sometimes members simply offer us this expression as a tool that has helped them. If we go back to our literature, we might be able to find some consolation in the original intent of this expression. Still, nothing says we have to accept each and every facet of our program. In Al-Anon each of us is free to take what we like and leave the rest. The Al-Anon tools are meant to benefit us, not do us harm. If we find that something doesn't work for us, we can keep looking until we find something else that does.

"Let Go and Let God" reminds us that we don't have to allow every passing feeling to take up permanent residence in us. We can allow whatever we are feeling to surface and subside. Knowing we don't have to be in pain every minute can give us some peace of mind. When we feel overwhelmed by any emotion, "One Day at a Time" reminds us that we only have to deal with today. Some days we may have to take life one hour or one minute at a time. Even if today ends up being full of nothing but sadness, we have little reason to believe that tomorrow will be the same. Our feelings can be powerful at times, but we don't have to let them control us.

If we're feeling stuck or confused, we can write about it. Many of us have found that putting our thoughts on paper leads to insights and clarity. The simple act of writing about our feelings has been healing for many of us. When our feelings seem to be crowding around us, writing them down can bring some order to what feels like chaos. Writing about our feelings does not have to be a formal activity, and we certainly don't have to consider ourselves "good" writers to do so. We can remember to "Keep It Simple." We may choose either to keep our writings private or share them with our Sponsor or close friend.

Whether we've been recovering for ten days or ten years, we all struggle from time to time when it comes to our feelings. One longtime member was surprised to find how hesitant she was to express her grief at meetings. She feared it would send the message to newcomers that the program doesn't work. Many of us have felt this same impulse to protect others from our feelings. When we give ourselves permission to feel our feelings without shame or guilt, we are taking an active role in our emotional healing. Instead of protecting others from our feelings, we become examples of how the Al-Anon program can work.

"I take comfort in knowing that my grief means I'm truly
dealing with my loss and am not in denial about it."

By facing our feelings, we stop running from ourselves. Although we may have once felt burdened by our emotions, today we trust that we'll be okay no matter what we feel. We may even come to feel gratitude for the gift of our feelings. After all, if we can't experience sadness, anger, or pain, how can we know joy, happiness, or serenity when it comes our way?

"I found a way to true happiness by being willing to deal with
my feelings instead of stuffing them."

Members share experience, strength, and hope: Dealing with our feelings

I learned a powerful lesson about grief and loss several years after joining Al-Anon. My cat of 16 years became terminally ill, and I made the decision to have her euthanized. My constant source of support since I was 13, she saw me through many difficult and lonely times as I faced the turmoil caused by alcoholism in my family. Until I found Al-Anon, my cat was often my only friend.

Losing her was devastating, and I left the veterinarian's office heartbroken. I knew I needed to be surrounded with love and support, but was afraid that if I spoke I would start crying. After all, I had been taught that, "Boys don't cry." I went to an open speaker's meeting, where I knew I could listen to encouragement and hope without having to say a word. After the meeting, I started to cry and managed to tell the man sitting next to me what had happened. This was a big step for me. I'll always remember his response. He said, "Whatever you do, don't ever let anyone convince you that it was 'just' a cat."

Through those words, I discovered that my feelings were valid and important. That simple sentence gave me permission to feel the way I did, whether others understood me or not. When I am in the throes of grief, not everyone will be able to relate to me, and even those who can relate may find it too painful to do so. What I learned that night was that other people's responses were none of my business. How they reacted to my feelings was not nearly as important as how I reacted to my feelings. I'm forever grateful for this awareness.

I have experienced many and varied losses in my life—from the death of my mother, to the emotional distancing of my siblings, to the estrangement of my teenage son. I dealt with my grief by stuffing my feelings and I soon became numb. I simply went on with my life, unaware of the cumulative effects of not recognizing, identifying, and working through my grief. Quite simply, I didn't know what I didn't know.

Since coming to Al-Anon, my grief has become more real. In the rooms and faces of Al-Anon, my Higher Power has given me a safe haven in which to feel. I may not always like how I feel, but I can now be aware of those feelings buried deep inside me for so long.

Before Al-Anon, my life was just about survival. Now I want to thrive. The day I walked into my first Al-Anon meeting was the day I was given all the tools I'll ever need. Keeping the focus on myself encourages me to become more acquainted with the real me. I now know I am exactly where I need to be, and I am forever grateful for the beautiful gift of being able to feel my feelings.

I wish I had known about Al-Anon 30 years ago. My mother died in a car accident after she had been drinking. For all those years, I lived with the guilt that somehow it was my fault. At the time, I didn't understand the disease of alcoholism or the effects it would have on my life. I had grown up in a home where only the alcoholics were allowed to express their feelings. I was so out of touch with my emotions, it would be 30 years before I could grieve or cry for my mother. I have always said that my mother died one day, and I went on with my life the next. I kept very tight control over my life, denying anything was wrong.

Eventually I was no longer able to control my life or deny my feelings, and I became filled with rage, anger, resentment, and bitterness. I was unequipped to handle these emotions. Someone suggested that I try Al-Anon. The most wonderful thing happened after only two meetings. I realized there were other people who had some of the same experiences I had. They accepted me with all my faults without judging me as bad. Al-Anon has given me so much in these past eight months. I have learned to reach out to other people and ask for help. I am developing a strong relationship with my Higher Power and am learning to surrender control of my life to Him. Al-Anon has helped open the door of forgiveness for myself and the alcoholics in my life. For all these things, I am tremendously grateful.

I lost my father when I was 19 years old, but it wasn't until I started Al-Anon ten years later that I was able to grieve that loss. Before Al-Anon, my grief came out indirectly.

My father made me director of our family business the year before he died. After his death, I was often late to board meetings, rude to staff, and generally unpleasant to be around. In Al-Anon I learned to check in with my feelings and reason things out with someone else—like my beloved Sponsor. With her help, I saw how much I missed my father, despite the difficulties his alcoholism caused. The board meetings made that loss more acute since he was so obviously absent.

I began writing about my feelings, sharing them with my Sponsor and at meetings, and taking extra special care of myself on board meeting days. Making use of these tools allowed me to acknowledge my grief, sadness, and anger without letting my feelings overwhelm me or lead me to behave inappropriately. I am so grateful to the program for giving me the skills to take care of myself and to better know myself. I now take pride in doing a good job as director of my father's company. I feel that being a good and responsible steward of his legacy is a way of honoring both him and me.

Recently at a meeting, someone raised the topic of grief and loss. I immediately became judgmental. In response to others sharing their feelings, I instructed all in attendance that grief was often self-indulgent and an exercise in "Me, me, me." When I left the meeting, I knew in my heart that I had been much too judgmental in taking everyone else's inventory.

Fortunately, life is a teacher, and it presented me with a lesson I had clearly not learned. My dog died. He was my constant companion and best friend of 13 years. It was then that I could see and feel grief and loss up close and personal. I could see it wasn't a mental exercise or problem to be analyzed. Rather, the experience put me in touch with my feelings. Thankfully I was able to share those feelings at the same home group where I had been so judgmental. Through that honest sharing, I was able to make amends to the members of my group. I now understand that I can't just bring my mind to meetings. I must also bring my heart.

While working the Steps, I realized I needed to make amends to my stepdaughter. I made plans to take her to lunch, hoping this could be the beginning of a new relationship.

The week before our lunch, she was killed in a car accident. I was so angry at God for depriving me of the opportunity to make amends to her.

During my grief, I received love and support from my Al-Anon friends. In time I realized that I could make a living amends by doing service work with the young members of Alateen. I could give them love, encouragement, and understanding, even if I couldn't do so for my stepdaughter.

I have learned that my Higher Power does have a plan for me. It might not be what I want or on my terms, but I can trust that I am being led exactly where I need to be.

I spent 55 years in denial. Denial that I was raised by a family of alcoholics. Denial that I was neglected by my parents. Denial that I married someone who also came from an alcoholic family. When my wife entered treatment for alcoholism, she challenged me to look at my part in our dysfunctional marriage. At first I balked. After all, denial had worked for me all my life. But I had been in a major depression that year, and I was looking for answers.

As I started going to Al-Anon meetings and working the program, I realized that I had passed on my behavioral deficiencies—taught to me by my parents—to my children. I also realized I had been critical and judgmental of my wife, all the time believing I was just making little jokes at her expense. Al-Anon helped me deal with the deep guilt I felt for the things I had done to my wife, my kids, and those around me.

I realized part of my depression was tied to the fact that everything I had been doing for the past 55 years to survive wasn't working. When I finally acknowledged this, I felt a huge sense of loss. I wasn't the person I thought I was—the one who could fix anything and everyone. I was, in fact, a caretaker, enmeshed in other people's lives, defining my happiness through my family's happiness. I felt I no longer had an identity. How could I have lied to myself all these years?

After reading an Al-Anon pamphlet, I realized it was time for me to take care of myself. How could I do this? My energy level was zero. The pamphlet said one way to practice caring for myself was to attend meetings. I could do that. The more meetings I attended, the better I felt. I'm still a newcomer to Al-Anon, but I've already learned so much. I know I still have anger inside me that I need to acknowledge in order to heal. I know Al-Anon is here to support me through it all.

My alcoholic father died when I was five years old. On the 25th anniversary of his death, I had a family portrait of him restored. My stepfather had cut my dad's face out of the picture in a drunken, jealous rage. In restoring the photo, I was able to find forgiveness for my stepfather, and I now had an image of my father to look at as I made amends. Finally I was able to grieve. I told my father how I missed him and wished he had been there to see me grow up. I forgave him for being less than perfect, since through the years I had learned that he was all too human.

My Sponsor told me that admitting I am powerless is the start of the grieving process. Eventually I was able to accept that I never had the dad I wanted, and the one I did get didn't love me in the way I wanted. I'm still grieving the loss of my dream for the perfect family.

Someone in the program told me that grief comes in waves, and I found this to be true. Every weekend, I set aside time to be alone, to feel, cry, write, and talk to my father. I'm finally allowing myself to feel the feelings I stuffed for 25 years. Members of my home group continue to reassure me that I'll be okay no matter how I feel, that "This too shall pass," and that I won't be grieving this loss forever.

Questions for reflection and meditation

- What did I learn about expressing emotions when I was growing up?
- Do I expect myself to change my feelings before I can accept myself for who I am?
- Which feelings are most difficult for me to express?
- What do I fear would happen if I allowed myself to express the feeling that I'm most uncomfortable with?
- Do I try to protect others from my feelings?
- Do I blame myself for any loss I've experienced?
- Is there an area of my life—past or present—in which I feel like a victim? What benefits do I receive from seeing myself in this way?
- If I've been angry at my Higher Power, what did I do—or what could I do—to resolve that situation?

Taking Care
of Ourselves

"Taking care of myself is something only I can do."

Before recovery, many of us struggled wi
take care of ourselves. We may have been a̲ᴜ̲.
to care for those around us, but we often didn't give oᴜ̲ɪ̲.
same consideration. In some cases, the ongoing emotional ana
physical caretaking we afforded others may have even contributed
to our own self-neglect. In the past, we may not have felt worthy
of our own attention. In Al-Anon we discover that taking care
of ourselves is not a luxury, but rather a vital part of our overall
health and recovery.

> *"After my spouse died, there was nothing I could do except take
> care of me."*

When we feel most powerless over our grief, there is still one
thing we do have some power over—taking care of ourselves.
Doing this while we are grieving might look different than at other
times. Most likely we will have different needs at this time. We
might want to increase our attendance at meetings or time with
our Sponsor so we can receive extra support. Letting others know
we are grieving, being honest about what we are feeling, and asking
for help are just a few more ways we can give ourselves care.

Some of us spent much of our lives believing that others knew
what was best for us. We may have dismissed our own intuition,
and instead looked to others to take care of us. The notion that
others are responsible for making us happy often left us feeling disappointed. In Al-Anon we learn to take responsibility for
ourselves, rather than expecting others to fulfill our needs. When
we commit to making our physical, emotional, and spiritual well-
being a priority, we set in motion a new course for our lives. We
can trust that we are capable of taking good care of ourselves,
even if we may have doubts about our ability to do so. Though we
may not have had good role models, it's never too late to learn.
Other Al-Anon members, who have both struggled and succeeded in caring for themselves, are there to help guide us. So is
our Higher Power.

Defining care for ourselves

Some of us have confused notions about taking care of ourselves, mistaking it for selfishness or self-pity. Such confusion can often lead us to feel guilty or unworthy when it comes to focusing on ourselves. Self-pity implies passivity and a feeling of helplessness about our lives. Selfishness implies caring *only* about our own needs with no regard for others. Taking care of ourselves means taking action to help ourselves feel better. It doesn't mean ignoring our responsibilities to others, but rather learning to balance those responsibilities while also putting ourselves in the equation.

If we were taught that other people's needs come first, the idea of putting ourselves first can leave us on shaky ground. If we've ever flown on an airplane, we're familiar with the safety instructions directing us to put on our own oxygen masks before assisting others. We may want to take a moment to consider these instructions, especially if we haven't given them much thought. Quite literally, if we weren't able to breathe, we couldn't be much help to anyone. As we practice taking care of ourselves, we eventually learn that it's possible to give to others in ways that don't compromise our own well-being.

What it means to take care of ourselves will vary from person to person. To relax, one person might prefer to take a nap or to curl up with a good book, while another might choose to go to the movies or to play a round of golf. If we're unsure how to take care of ourselves at first, we can start by considering what we might do to help a close friend, and try that. We can experiment until we discover what feels right for us.

Initially our desire to please others may be stronger than our desire to take care of ourselves. Sometimes caring for ourselves means putting the needs of others on hold. As we practice any new behavior, others may react negatively or with hurt feelings. After all, they may not be used to seeing us put ourselves first.

Our compassion for others can sometimes make it difficult to set limits. We don't have to let other people's reactions dictate whether or not we take care of ourselves. We can learn to set boundaries and allow others to have their feelings without believing we're responsible for them.

If we're feeling guilty about giving ourselves attention, we can remind ourselves that this is a feeling that will pass as we become more comfortable with ourselves. Many of us have found that as we learn to love ourselves and as our self-esteem increases, our feelings of guilt will lessen. Al-Anon's slogan "Live and Let Live" can help if we are feeling guilty. Often we focus on the "Let Live" part of this slogan, and not enough on the "Live" part. We need to live too. To live well, we must treat ourselves well.

Some days we may not want to take care of ourselves, or we might not have the energy to do so. Simply being aware of how we are feeling is one way we can take care of ourselves. We don't always have to be doing some activity to practice taking care of ourselves. Maybe we need to spend the day in our pajamas, doing nothing. Being gentle with ourselves is part of caring for ourselves too. We can give ourselves a break when we need it.

The more we practice the Al-Anon principles, the more we learn to trust our intuition—that small voice inside that lets us know what we need. There are no small acts when it comes to taking care of ourselves. When we aren't sure what we need, we can turn to the wealth of resources available to us in Al-Anon.

Asking for help

> *"Anytime, day or night, I know I can reach out for the help of Al-Anon. It has always been there for me. All I have to do is ask."*

Each of us admitted we needed help when we walked into our first Al-Anon meeting. Still, many of us are uncomfortable with the idea of asking for help. If we regard ourselves as independent and self-sufficient, we may believe that asking for help is a sign of weakness.

We hear a lot about humility in Al-Anon. To be humble suggests that we are still teachable. It means we haven't figured everything out for ourselves, and that we are open to learning. Admitting that we need other people requires an attitude of humility. Asking for help takes courage, and as most of us can probably agree, courage is a sign of strength, not weakness. We weren't meant to take this journey called life by ourselves. It's okay to ask for help.

"Al-Anon carried me when I could not carry myself."

In the past, we may have expected others to know what we needed without having to ask. In Al-Anon we learn how to be more direct in communicating our needs. Once we learn how to ask for help, we may still struggle with allowing ourselves to accept the help offered to us. Part of being in healthy relationships means learning to receive. We don't always have to be the giver. It's okay to let ourselves receive without worrying about how to return the favor. When we ask for help, we present others with the opportunity to give. Many of us have found that when we ask for help and allow ourselves to receive, our relationships strengthen and deepen. After all, how can we ever know true friendship if we never let others see our vulnerabilities?

"The great thing about people in Al-Anon is they know how to help when asked, without trying to 'fix.'"

We may find it easier to ask for help from Al-Anon members than from other people in our lives. There are countless ways we can reach out for help. We can let others in our group know we are in need. We can turn to our Sponsor if we have one. If we are new to the program, we can ask someone to talk with us after a meeting. We can go for coffee with other members, where we have the chance to share more about what we are going through. At times asking for help might be as basic as picking up the phone.

Once we take the risk and ask for what we need, it can be difficult to let go of the outcome. There will most likely be occasions when others will say no to our request for help. We don't have to take it personally if someone else is unable or unwilling to be there for us at the very moment we ask. That person might not be able to help for a variety of reasons which have nothing to do with us. We don't have to give up when someone says no. We can ask someone else. If that person also says no, we can keep asking until we find someone who says yes.

Tending to our physical, emotional, and spiritual well-being

There is no one right way to care for ourselves. What it means to take care of ourselves will be different for each of us. We can start by looking at those aspects of ourselves we may have been neglecting—whether physical, emotional, or spiritual. Caring for ourselves while we are grieving is critical to our healing. Even if we've become masters at caring for ourselves, we can find ourselves slipping while in the midst of grief. Some days we might forget to eat or exercise. We might stop attending meetings or reaching out to others, or we may find it difficult to pray or meditate.

If we are feeling confused about what we need, we can keep it simple by asking ourselves if we are hungry, angry, lonely, or tired. One member allowed herself what she called "do-nothing days" and "cry days." If we are feeling stressed, we can soak in a hot bath or treat ourselves to a massage. Discovering what interests us and what brings us joy is another way we can care for ourselves. We might decide to learn something new or take up a hobby we've always wanted to try.

It's hard to separate our physical, emotional, and spiritual well-being from each other. All are parts of the whole that is us. When one part is fed, all are nourished. Yet if one part is neglected, all can become out of balance. As we grow more comfortable tending to our basic needs, we may find it easier to branch out and try new ways of taking care of ourselves. Making time each day to check in with ourselves—even if it's only for a few minutes—allows us to see what kind of attention we most need. The following list might help if we are not sure where to begin:

- Am I nurturing my body by eating right, exercising, and getting plenty of rest?
- Am I taking time for myself and participating in activities I enjoy?
- Am I honoring my feelings?
- Am I allowing myself whatever time I need to grieve?
- Am I able to ask for help?
- Am I spending time in daily prayer and meditation with my Higher Power?
- Am I getting to enough meetings?
- Am I reaching out to my Sponsor or other Al-Anon friends?
- Am I making use of Al-Anon literature when I can't get to meetings or talk with someone?

We would most likely feel overwhelmed if we had to tend to all our needs at once. This is not about perfection; it's about making the effort to treat ourselves better.

We can expect to feel uncomfortable when we first start taking care of ourselves. Some of us might question whether we should be using our time and resources to benefit others instead of ourselves. We can remind ourselves that we have a right to treat ourselves well. Most new behaviors feel uncomfortable at first. Much like strengthening a muscle, we may feel discomfort in the beginning. Though just as with exercise, the more we practice taking care of ourselves, the easier it becomes.

Turning to our Higher Power

"Since coming to Al-Anon, I've learned that grief and God go together."

Prayer and meditation have gotten many of us through our toughest hours when we felt most powerless and afraid. Many of us find it helpful to practice a daily routine of prayer and meditation. We might choose to pray or meditate first thing in the morning before we get out of bed, or we might spend time in reflection before we go to sleep. Others pray throughout the day. If we have a particular religious affiliation, we might recite formal prayers that reflect our faith. We might be more spontaneous and relaxed about how we pray or meditate. Taking a walk in nature, looking at a painting, reading a poem that draws us inward, feeding the birds in our backyard, or caring for the plants in our garden— these are just a few ways we can nurture our spirits. Fortunately there is more than one way to lead a spiritual life. We can choose whatever helps us feel renewed daily.

The awareness of a Power greater than ourselves has helped many of us feel less alone in our grief. One member discovered that her loneliness presented her with the opportunity to spend more time with her Higher Power. During our most intense moments of grief, our vulnerability can become the doorway through which we invite our Higher Power more fully into our lives. Some prayers have words, and some are silent. Perhaps the type of prayer or length of time spent in meditation is not nearly as important as making the effort to connect with our Higher Power.

"At times, the only prayer I could say was 'God help me.'"

How the Steps can help

"Just recalling the Steps gives me the strength and courage to move forward."

Many of us have found healing and serenity when we put the Steps to use in our daily lives. The Twelve Steps are fundamental to the Al-Anon program and essential to our recovery. They help us better understand ourselves so we can make peace with our past and learn how to live in the present. The Steps teach us about acceptance, humility, forgiveness, and taking care of ourselves. We can apply one of the Steps to almost any problem or situation we might be facing. Each time we work the Steps, we discover new aspects of ourselves.

Because each Step builds upon the previous one, some of us find it helpful to take the Steps in order. Once we become more familiar with them, we can choose to go back and see how one or two Steps might help us with a particular aspect of our grief. To learn more about how the Steps can help us, we can read about them in our literature or attend Step meetings. Some of us find it helpful to spend time meditating on a Step or writing about it. While grieving, one member used the Twelve Steps as a form of walking meditation, concentrating on a different Step each lap around the track.

We don't have to wander aimlessly through our grief. If we feel lost or off-course, we can turn to the Steps. They can provide us with structure and stability when our grief feels overwhelming and our lives seem out of control. As we grow and change, so too will our understanding of the Steps. Fortunately we can journey through them as often as we need.

Making use of the slogans

A member described just how indispensable one particular slogan is to him as follows: "'One Day at a Time' is not an overused phrase; it's my way of life." We hear the slogans referred to so often that we may rarely stop to actually consider what they have to offer. If some of our slogans seem a bit clichéd to us, our tendency might be to dismiss them. But the simplicity of our slogans is what makes them so effective. In the midst of our grief, a slogan may be the only Al-Anon tool we have the energy to use. If we are having a hard time focusing our attention, we can simply turn to the slogans.

Al-Anon slogans and phrases are quick reminders for us to stop whatever we are doing and focus on some aspect of taking care of ourselves. "Keep It Simple" can help us during those times when our grief seems unmanageable. "Easy Does It" can help us slow down and be gentle with ourselves. When fears about the future bombard us, "One Day at a Time" and "Let Go and Let God" can help us focus on this day, this moment.

"First Things First" can be a helpful reminder, especially at those times when it feels like we might not make it through the day. "This slogan reminds me to stop and think about what needs to be done first, instead of spinning out of control trying to do everything at once and getting nothing done," one member said. We can also use this slogan as a way to check in with ourselves to see what we might need at any given moment—a nap, a meeting, a walk with a trusted friend, a phone call with a member of our group or our Sponsor, time to ourselves, or a good cry. We can trust that if we ask for guidance, our Higher Power will give us exactly what we need.

Our slogans can help calm us when we are anxious. They can keep our minds from spinning out of control. One member found it helpful to use the slogans as a mantra, repeating each phrase in between deep breaths. If we haven't given much thought to the slogans lately, we might want to take some time to reacquaint ourselves with them. We can refer to almost any piece of our literature to read more about the slogans. Suggesting a particular slogan as a topic at a meeting can also help us learn how others have benefited from using the slogans.

Attending meetings

When we first walked into the rooms of Al-Anon, many of us felt a tremendous sense of comfort. One member shared that it felt like being wrapped in a warm blanket. We often find that we can breathe more deeply in the company of others who know what we are going through. In the past, we may have tried to share our problems with friends, colleagues, or neighbors, only to feel pitied or misunderstood. In Al-Anon we may have been surprised and relieved when we realized we didn't have to explain ourselves to anyone. Instead, we found a unique kinship with others who understood because they shared the same struggles. Just realizing we were not alone was a great source of comfort to so many of us.

A meeting might be the only safe place we have where we can speak from our hearts. If our home lives are chaotic and stressful, however, we may worry that if we go to a meeting, we may come home to an even worse situation. We can trust that we will be in a better position to deal with whatever awaits us at home because we took care of ourselves by getting to a meeting.

> *"I put on a good front for the world, believing my sorrow was*
> *too personal to share."*

If we have issues with trust or shame, we may not feel comfortable opening up to strangers right away. Those of us who have kept the secret of alcoholism for so long may need some time until we are comfortable enough to talk about our problems. Some of us may have been deeply hurt in the past by others who ignored us or dismissed our feelings. As a result, we may have convinced ourselves we have nothing of value to offer. For those of us who have struggled in this way, we may find it especially difficult to voice our innermost thoughts at a meeting. It might take months for some of us to just say our name.

> *"I came into the rooms so sad and broken that for many months*
> *I couldn't speak."*

We don't ever have to feel pressure to share at a meeting if we don't want to or if we are not ready. Even if we never utter a word, our presence can benefit the group in ways we may never fully know. To share means to give something of ourselves. Being fully present and actively listening is also a form of sharing. Listening to others can also help us become more aware of our own feelings. One day, we might feel comfortable enough to share something, even if it's only to say we are glad to be at a meeting. In time, we might even feel safe enough to tell our story.

> *"I have to keep sharing even when I'm tired of hearing myself talk about my losses, and even when I'm worried that other people are sick of listening."*

Fear of what others might think of us can keep us from opening up at meetings. It's no one's job to sit in judgment of how we are grieving. Some meetings will be a better fit for us than others. We owe it to ourselves to find the meetings that are right for us, where we feel supported.

If we struggle with low self-esteem, we may have convinced ourselves that no one wants to listen to what we have to say, even if we have no evidence from others in our group. When we take the risk to share more deeply, we might be surprised to find that others *want* to hear what we have to say. While his mother was dying, one member frequently shared how much her physical pain was affecting him: "After each meeting, I always expected someone to say something like, 'Do you think you could take a break from talking about your mom next week?' Instead I heard, 'This too will pass,' and 'I've been where you are. Here's my number; please call.'" Recognizing that others can benefit from what we have to say helps build our self-esteem.

Meetings provide us with the opportunity to connect with other Al-Anon members face-to-face. We would limit ourselves if we only sought out people who are going through exactly what we are. We might be surprised to find that we have as much to learn from a newcomer as from a longtime member. Even if someone's experience seems unlike our own, we just might discover beneath the details of our lives how much we have in common.

By attending meetings on a regular basis, we invite the possibility of change into our lives. Sometimes that means getting ourselves to a meeting even when we don't want to go. It's often when we want to skip a meeting that we need it the most. It can help if we remind ourselves that we usually leave feeling better than when we arrived. Some days we may barely feel like getting out of bed, much less getting dressed and going to a meeting. In Al-Anon we don't ever have to pretend we are doing any better than we are. We can be assured that we will be welcomed and accepted, no matter how we're dressed or how we're feeling.

Keep coming back

> *"There's something more than my own weak will that keeps me*
> *coming back to Al-Anon."*

Many of us keep coming back to meetings long after the problems that first led us to Al-Anon have been resolved or no longer bother us. Most of us agree that the longer we are in Al-Anon, the more the program can help us in all areas of our lives—not just those related to alcoholism. Al-Anon is not a program of completion or destination. The tools we gain here help us lead healthier lives—in our work, in our relationships with family and friends, and in our love relationships. Meetings are available throughout the world. If we know we are going to be out of town, we can find a meeting in that area.

> *"When things get tough, I can always count on Al-Anon to be*
> *there for me, whether I'm at home or a 1,000 miles away."*

How we approach our relationship to the Al-Anon program will most likely change over time. As we grow, our needs will naturally change. Some of us attend the same meetings each week for years.

Others like to try new meetings where we can hear different per-spectives. There is no one right way to be an Al-Anon member, just as there is no one right way to grieve. As mentioned in the Suggested Al-Anon/Alateen Closing statement read at the end of each meeting, "Take what you like and leave the rest." Each of us is entitled to find our own relationship to Al-Anon—the one that is right for us.

How sponsorship can help

While at meetings, we try to be mindful of leaving enough time for all who would like to share. Therefore we may not always have the opportunity to express all that's in our hearts and minds. There may also be certain issues in our lives that we don't feel comfortable sharing at meetings. In such instances, we can find help through sponsorship.

Sponsorship provides us with the opportunity to have more in-depth conversations in a one-on-one setting with someone we trust. Having a Sponsor available to us when we are grieving can be especially valuable. When we feel most alone, we can count on our Sponsor to be there for us. We can call our Sponsor when we feel confused or overwhelmed, or when we need some extra sup-port and understanding.

"Grief and loss were just two words in my vocabulary until my
Sponsor helped me through the loss of my mother."

For many of us, it was the encouragement and support we received from our Sponsor that got us through the toughest moments of our grief. Over time many of us come to feel that our Sponsor knows us better than anyone, perhaps even better than our families. Though our Sponsor won't have all the answers, he or she can often help guide us to the answers that lie within us.

When we agree to sponsor someone, we may not be aware of

how much we will end up receiving. Many members have found that the person they sponsor had much to teach them about themselves too. Often the concerns brought to us as Sponsors are the very things we are ready to examine in ourselves. None of us arrives at a place where we've learned all there is to learn. If we stay open-minded, we will find that insights from other members can help us, no matter how long we—or they—have been recovering.

If we are sponsoring someone while we are grieving, we will need to determine for ourselves if we can continue our role as Sponsor, or if we need to take a break for a while. This can be a difficult decision to make, especially if we are sponsoring a newcomer. We can remind ourselves that the key to another's recovery does not lie within us. In fact, by taking care of ourselves, we become a living example of how to put the Al-Anon principles into practice. What better gift could we offer the person we are sponsoring?

Growth through service

"I don't know how helping someone else helps me. I only know that it does."

Service is not a required activity of Al-Anon members. We give only when we truly want to or feel called to give—not out of guilt, obligation, or pressure. We need each other to recover, and Twelfth Step work such as service is one way we can be there for each other. Service can be an occasion to allow our grief to rest for a short time as we listen to another person or focus on a specific task.

"One way I can serve is by honestly sharing my experiences and feelings. Whatever I need to say, chances are there is someone else who benefits from hearing it."

Service can mean sponsoring a newcomer, making coffee, setting up literature, greeting people as they arrive at a meeting, or helping to clean up afterwards. Carrying the message to others can mean simply offering our phone number to someone in need or sharing our experience of grief. The truth is, we may never truly know how our earned wisdom might help someone who is struggling. Even if we fear we don't have anything to give while we are grieving, the smallest act of generosity can go a long way toward helping someone else—and ourselves.

Some of us are willing and able to accept service positions that involve a good deal of our time and energy, such as Group or District Representative. Though not all areas of service require the same level of commitment, each is equally important and valuable in Al-Anon. Something as simple as being the first to arrive and unlock the door assures that the meeting will take place. Taking a moment to be sure that meeting schedules are readily available can make it easier for the newcomer who might be too nervous to ask for one.

> *"When I felt like I couldn't get through another day, I could*
> *hear my Sponsor's voice saying, 'If you don't know what*
> *to do, do something.' I knew there was always something I*
> *could do in Al-Anon."*

Many of us have found healing and gratitude through service. Twelfth Step work has helped us feel more a part of our group and of Al-Anon as a whole. It connects us with others and often leads to lasting friendships. Service can help us feel wanted, needed, and loved. It can help us gain confidence and self-esteem. The more we know ourselves, the more we have of ourselves to give. For many of us, service gives us the opportunity to be seen for who we are and for the unique gifts we have to offer. One member shared how a service position helped him feel less alone in his grief.

> *"Within a few short weeks, my life had gone from loss and*
> *emptiness to more fullness than I could have ever imagined."*

Certain service positions require time and energy we may not have to give while we are grieving. In such cases, we can remind ourselves that we have choices. Some of us choose to stay in our service roles because we don't want to feel isolated. A service commitment can motivate us to show up at a meeting, even when we don't feel like going. Service can also help us get out of our heads and can give us temporary reprieve from our own troubles. If our service commitment becomes too much for us at this time, we can take a break and resume our duties when we feel ready. If we're not sure, we can continue with the awareness that we can step aside if it becomes more than we can handle.

Reading our literature

Al-Anon Conference Approved Literature contains a wealth of experience and wisdom from thousands of members all over the world. That experience and wisdom is available to each of us, day or night. The collective sharing of so many members can serve as hopeful reminders that we are not alone, and that we too can survive our losses. If we can't sleep or if it's too late to call our Sponsor, we can turn to our literature. When others are unavailable or we can't get to a meeting, we can find comfort in its pages. Those days when we don't feel like talking to anyone, our literature can be a quiet friend who asks nothing from us in return.

Perhaps the most wonderful thing about our literature is that we can take it with us anywhere. We might also choose to write down certain phrases and post them on our refrigerator, mirror, or other places we pass by each day. When returning to work seemed momentous for one member, she found comfort in reading the *Just for Today* bookmark before the start of each workday.

> *"Each day felt like a hurdle that was too high for me to jump. Those words helped me focus on just that one day ahead of me. It was like my Higher Power was giving me a daily dose of spiritual vitamins through the words on that bookmark. It might sound dramatic, but I felt like that bookmark saved my life during that difficult time."*

We can find readings in most of our literature that will speak to almost any aspect of our grief. One member shared, "God's will is not left up to my imagination, thank goodness. Otherwise, I would bypass important healing messages." Some members ask their Higher Power to lead them to a passage that will help. Others trust their intuition, opening to a page spontaneously. If we don't find something right away, we can keep looking, or turn to another book or pamphlet until we find something that gives us comfort.

Many of us consider the use of Al-Anon literature to be an important component of our spiritual practice. As we grow in our recovery, we might find that the same piece of literature can offer us new insights upon subsequent readings. In this way, our Al-Anon literature helps reflect our progress.

In the midst of our grief, reading even one page may take all the energy we can muster. Yet even this small step is a powerful act of taking care of ourselves. Just by seeking out and reading some part of this book, we have already taken an important step toward lessening our pain and healing from our grief.

Members share experience, strength, and hope: Taking care of ourselves

When I entered the rooms of Al-Anon, I was newly married to an alcoholic. I was so focused on my husband that I was completely ignoring my own diabetes. While I cringed at the thought of spending money on equipment to check my glucose levels, I was happy to purchase whatever my husband needed or wanted.

Soon after I started attending Al-Anon, I began to suffer from complications due to my diabetes. My sight, which was already impaired, became much worse, and I had to stop driving. I was 28 years old, yet it seemed like my life was over. I felt hopeless in my grief. To make matters worse, I had a hard time asking for help.

I wasn't really close to program friends, and I wondered how I would get to meetings. I finally decided I had to ask for help. At first it was excruciating for me, but as time went on, it became easier. Al-Anon helped me understand that my value is not in being an island.

The Seventh Tradition has been a valuable tool that saved my life and my sanity. I discovered that being "self-supporting," as this Tradition instructs, does not mean doing it all by myself. It means doing as much as I can healthily do and asking for help with the rest. It also means letting others help me.

When my husband was diagnosed with incurable cancer, I quit the job I'd held for 32 years so I could take care of him. Soon after his death, my sister became disabled as a result of her long-term addictions. Our parents, in their mid-80s, were doing their best to take care of her. In fact, they were so preoccupied with trying to fix her, they began neglecting their own needs. I was overwhelmed by the loss of my husband and my job, and by worrying about my parents and my sister. I felt guilty because I couldn't seem to make things better for them. I was terrified about the future, which I pictured as an endless ordeal of caretaking, crises, and bereavements. I didn't see how I was going to manage without my husband by my side. I even thought about shooting myself with his shotgun, except I couldn't figure out how to load it.

Finally it occurred to me to look for an Al-Anon group. I'd been thinking about joining for years, but kept making excuses about not having enough time or not wanting people to know about my family's problems. This time, however, I had to admit that my life truly had become unmanageable, and I didn't know where else to turn.

What I found was a room full of people whose difficulties were like mine, but who seemed to be figuring out how to live well in spite of them. They made me feel welcome and listened to me without judging or giving advice. Today these new friends are showing me by example how to direct my attention to the one person I can actually do something about: me. I am learning how to live "One Day at a Time," instead of always dreading the future or longing for the past. I am learning how to detach with love from my family's problems. When I think about turning my life over to a Higher Power, it seems like life without my husband might be livable after all. Though I'm still a beginner in Al-Anon, I've already been able to see how the program has saved my life.

Before Al-Anon, I hated my father and had nothing but contempt for his every breath. He ruined our family, having chosen alcohol over us. After the death of my mother, my father was completely lost. My mother used to do everything for him. He didn't cook, clean, pay the bills, wash the car, or mow the lawn. Her death sent him into a guilt-ridden depression from which he would never recover.

One night I stopped by to bring my father dinner. As I entered the dark house, I found him in a drunken stupor on the couch. I said the Serenity Prayer and put his food in the refrigerator. He woke as I was leaving. "I'm drunk," he said. I responded that I loved him. As I turned to leave he yelled out, "Are you just going to leave me here like this?" My answer was yes, and I quietly shut the door and drove home. I had never done anything like that before. Not taking care of him felt uncomfortable. I cried all the way home, feeling guilty at what a horrible son I was. Once home, I called an Al-Anon friend and told him what happened. "You did exactly what you were supposed to do," he reassured me. "Pray about it and get some rest."

I later realized I had taken the First Step and released my father to God. "Live and Let Live" came to mind, along with an intense sense of compassion for my father. That evening changed everything between my dad and me. We became closer as I set boundaries with him, and we talked like never before. He was sober for only five months before he died. But with the help of Al-Anon, it was five months I never thought I would have with my dad.

———————————

It was my own response to the alcoholism in my family that led me to seek help from Al-Anon. It seemed I was the unhappy one—not my mother, father, grandparents, or any of the other alcoholics in my life. Over time I began to practice the Al-Anon principles, and I started to build a life that felt satisfying and contented. As my mother's alcoholism continued to worsen, it became clear that in order to maintain peace in my life, I would have to distance myself from her. For several years, my mother and I saw little of each other.

When I learned that my mother was dying, the little girl in me wanted to run to her side. I was in a state of inner turmoil to the point of falling ill myself. During this time, I went to meetings, prayed earnestly to the God of my understanding, and leaned on my friends. Yet no answer came as to what I should do.

One day during my meditative time, it became suddenly clear. "First Things First" repeatedly kept coming to mind. That's when I became aware that my mother's impending death was far more important than any of her past alcoholic behavior. With this slogan in mind, I was able to set new priorities. I made the choice to be with my mother and help care for her through the final weeks of her illness. In the time we had together, we developed a new relationship based on honesty, amends, and love. I was able to find forgiveness in my heart.

I am grateful for the clarity that came to me that day while meditating. My daily Eleventh Step helped me see how I could apply the Al-Anon principles to this baffling and difficult situation. It helped me make the decision that felt right for me.

———————————

I recently chose to separate from my wife because our relationship was threatening my recovery, not to mention my serenity. I am still very sad about the separation and mourn the death of a relationship that began with such promise.

Despite having left home, I still find myself worrying about how my wife will react to certain situations. At other times, I feel sad because I left a nice house for a rundown two-room apartment. The temptation to wallow in self-pity or anxiety can be very strong at times. This is where my program kicks in. I pray; I sit down and journal; I pick up the phone. I'm amazed at how often an Al-Anon friend will call at exactly the right time. Listening to another member's story helps me get out of my head.

I'm often reminded that feelings aren't facts, and that I have choices. One thing I can do is apply the slogans to my thoughts and feelings. "Easy Does It" allows me to go through these difficult days at my own pace, not how someone else says it should be. "Live and Let Live" gives my wife the right to live her own life without my judging her. "One Day at a Time" reminds me to stay out of a regret-filled past or a frightening future. I have only today to deal with. When the pain, loneliness, and uncertainty seem too much to bear, I gently repeat the phrase "This too shall pass" to remind myself that even this will not last.

My greatest grief came as a result of ending a five-year relationship. I felt as if my entire being had suffered wounds that would never heal. I began going to Al-Anon meetings within the first week of ending the relationship. I didn't know at the time how much attending meetings would assist me in my grief.

That first desperate week, the slogans were my lifesaver. I could barely hear the words spoken by fellow members, but the slogans, which were always placed on the table at that particular meeting, gave me hope—hope that just maybe I could accept this loss and let go of my sense of failure. My shame was compounded from being a lesbian and having to deal with social ostracism. I had a hard time being able to see and accept the loving person beneath the shame. The slogans, the other Al-Anon members, and the structure of the meetings helped me to eventually feel safe enough to peel away the layers and to discover that I am both loving and worthy of being loved.

My time in Al-Anon has taught me how to trust my instincts. Never was this clearer to me than when I was grieving my brother's suicide. The morning of his funeral, I knew I needed the safety and comfort of an Al-Anon meeting. It wasn't my regular meeting day, so I found a different meeting.

Once there, I knew there was another reason I had come. My years in the program have taught me that fear and pain can be diminished by sharing them. I knew I needed to share what was happening in my life. It took some time for me to get the courage to say it out loud, but finally I opened up and shared that I was there because my brother had killed himself, that his funeral was that afternoon, and I couldn't stand the pain.

The comfort and support I received that day is something I cannot begin to describe. I have never understood why telling a trusted listener about something horrible somehow makes it less horrifying, but for me, it does. I will always be grateful to those Al-Anon members that morning who gave me the strength to face the rest of the day.

I was attending Al-Anon meetings on a weekly basis, but I wasn't using the program to help me deal with my losses. I had no Sponsor, and my program had weakened over the years. I was dealing with my feelings just as I had learned to in my alcoholic home—by myself. I grew more and more isolated and distant.

In my grief, help came to me through a channel I had not anticipated: service. For years my home group was without a Group Representative. One evening I was asked to fill that role. I felt I needed to grow in my program and believed my Higher Power was leading me to service, so I said yes. Within a few short weeks, I had gone from almost total isolation in my grief to an expanded sense of fellowship. Over time I began to participate in more and more service activities, and eventually I became a Sponsor. Service has taught me that I help myself by helping others. My life today is fuller than I could have ever imagined.

I love sponsoring, but when my mother died, I found I could not be there for the individuals I was sponsoring. Someone I trust suggested I take a hiatus from sponsoring for one year so I could take care of me. I was very concerned about my sponsees and wondered where they would turn. Finally I had to trust that they would be taken care of. I called my sponsees and told them I would be taking a year off from sponsoring so I could take care of myself through my grief.

I always thought the Al-Anon saying "When I got busy, I got better" would apply to grief, but for me, just the opposite was true. I needed time to myself for a while in order to heal. I attended meetings, sometimes leaving early to avoid talking to others. I even went to meetings where I didn't know anyone. I just couldn't be around my close Al-Anon friends during this painful time. I like to say that year was my time to cocoon.

My decision to take time away from sponsoring was probably the hardest but best thing I could have done for myself. That year was a very intimate, sad, and healing time—one I didn't even realize I needed. I'm so grateful I took care of myself, and I believe it has enhanced my relationships with my sponsees today. I thank my Higher Power every day for this program and for the wisdom of those who have walked before me. I don't know how I would have healed otherwise.

Questions for reflection and meditation

- How have I tended to my physical well-being today?
- What can I do today to help myself feel better emotionally?
- Do I have a regular time reserved for meetings, prayer, and meditation?
- What can I do to help myself feel better spiritually?
- Can I recognize a tendency to isolate myself instead of finding support that could help me?
- At this time in my life, what opportunity for Al-Anon service would be best suited to my need for recovery, one step at a time?

Spiritual Growth from Grieving

"When I found Al-Anon, nothing changed but me."

Life provides us with numerous opportunities to grow spiritually. For many of us, grief can be such an opportunity. We may be unaware, however, of the spiritual gifts that can come from grieving, especially if we are in the midst of it. The awareness of such gifts often comes much later. Whether facing the loss of a loved one, a marriage, a close relationship, our childhood, or our dreams, healing from grief of such magnitude may have once seemed impossible to us. Nevertheless, it is through our grief that many of us have found deeper and more meaningful lives.

The spiritual gifts that come from grieving are often subtle, but they become more apparent as we reflect on the ways we've grown and changed. Even if our lives might not look dramatically different, we find that they feel different because we have changed. By focusing on ourselves and letting go of expectations, we no longer react in the ways we once did. One day we may find ourselves responding calmly to a situation that would have once upset us for days. Instead of looking to others to take care of us, we now look to ourselves. When we pray, we ask for strength, courage, and wisdom, rather than for specific outcomes.

"I have been blessed to be able to sit with my own pain and grief
in a way that has changed my life."

In Al-Anon we become willing to learn more about ourselves as we strive to heal from our painful pasts. Most of all, we find hope in the midst of our despair. That hope has come through Al-Anon. Knowing that we don't have to face our grief alone gives many of us the courage to face life again. We discover that healing from our grief is possible because we have seen it happen for others. Being in recovery doesn't mean our lives will be problem-free. We can take comfort, however, in knowing that with Al-Anon's help, we are better equipped to handle whatever challenges come our way.

Increased self-awareness and self-esteem

Our work in Al-Anon has helped many of us come to a deeper understanding of ourselves. In making a commitment to deepen and strengthen our relationship with a Higher Power on a daily basis, we soon find that we're growing and changing spiritually. We have so much to be proud of. We have worked hard and persisted, even when we felt like giving up. By applying the tools of the program to our lives, we become free from the burdens and fears that once held us back. For many, this newfound freedom gives us a new outlook on life.

In the past, focusing on others and neglecting our own needs caused many of us to lose ourselves to the disease of alcoholism. Where we once may have felt trapped in our lives, today we recognize that we have choices. Now, rather than focusing on changing the alcoholic, we focus on changing ourselves.

"Without the program, I'd still be blaming, rationalizing, and manipulating the alcoholic to do what I thought was best."

Before Al-Anon, we may not have known what it was like to take care of ourselves during times of struggle. By learning to focus on ourselves, we grow in self-awareness and self-esteem. We come to realize that we are deserving of our own attention and that we are worthy of love and respect. By learning to put the focus on himself, one member noticed how much he had changed: "Today, rather than praying for an end to active alcoholism in my home, I pray that the alcoholics in my life will know the serenity and inner confidence that has come to me." For many of us, our grief can help us know ourselves more fully. When we strive to make peace with our pasts, we can begin to build new relationships and to find forgiveness for the alcoholics, our families, and ourselves.

Today we can trust ourselves to know what's best for us without having to live up to anyone else's standards. As we grow in self-esteem, we come to appreciate what makes us unique. Each of us brings something to Al-Anon that no one else can—ourselves. If we were all the same, we wouldn't have much to gain from each other's experiences. It's our individual uniqueness that makes it possible for us to learn from one another.

Letting go and moving on

Experience teaches us that grief does not happen in a linear way. Rather, it tends to ebb and flow much like waves on the ocean. When it comes to grieving, we don't reach an imaginary finish line. If a loved one has died, we may wonder if we will be abandoning them by moving on with our lives. We may fear that if we let go of our old hopes and dreams, we won't have anything to take their place. These fears are natural enough. When we let go of our old dreams, we may need to stand in a place of not knowing for a while. This in-between place may feel uncomfortable, yet it is often the place where we can begin to build new dreams. It is this place of not knowing that, for many of us, becomes an integral part of our spiritual growth.

"I'm still grieving, but the despair is gone."

In moving forward, we can accept our losses and learn to live with our grief. When we reach this point, many of us become aware of the spiritual lessons that can come from grieving. Moving forward doesn't mean we forget about our losses or that we are through with our grief. We may always feel some degree of sadness and pain over certain losses, but with acceptance, we find that the pain lessens over time. Eventually, we will feel ready to let go and move on. We can trust ourselves to know when that time has come.

"I am learning that though I grieve incredibly for the loss of my marriage and for the loss of my children's father, I don't have to drown in that pain."

Reflecting on our progress

"Looking back, I can still experience the pain I once felt. But it's the looking back that tells me how I have grown."

It's easy to become focused on the next learning experience, the next challenge. Though we may want to keep moving forward, we can benefit from pausing periodically to reflect on our progress. Step Twelve refers to "having had a spiritual awakening as a result of these steps . . . ." It can give us the opportunity to reflect on how we've changed. We recall where we were at the onset of our grief and acknowledge where we are today.

Step Twelve is not only about our own changes. One member came to realize that Step Twelve is about more than creating a better life for himself; it is also about encouraging and helping others. When we share our struggles and the changes we've made, we inspire others and offer hope that healing from our grief is possible.

"Thanks to Al-Anon, I have done more than just survive. I have emerged as a stronger, more loving, and more compassionate human being."

Gratitude

"After the acute pain of grief, the one feeling at the forefront now is gratitude—tremendous, overwhelming gratitude."

When we first come to Al-Anon, it can be hard to imagine that we could feel anything but contempt for a disease that has caused us so much suffering and grief. For many of us, however, alcoholism becomes a catalyst for growth and change, ultimately leading us to a place of gratitude. We may even feel grateful for the alcoholic in our lives, without whom we may have never found Al-Anon.

"It took the experiences with active alcoholism for me to know the peace I've found in the program. Life today is much different than I had ever anticipated."

It could be said that gratitude is the cornerstone of our recovery. Without it, we would most likely give up hope for a better life. Although we may once have felt dread about the future, we now begin to feel excitement about the possibility for change in our lives and the lessons that will help make those changes. When we slip into old ways of behaving or when we make a mistake, we can choose to see it as an opportunity to learn something about ourselves, rather than as an opportunity to shame ourselves.

Gratitude doesn't mean we have to feel happy about everything that's happening in our lives. "I can't say I'm grateful for the loss of my marriage," one member said, "but I can say I'm grateful for the many lessons I've learned from it." Another member had this to say: "My eyes have been opened to gifts in my life that I wouldn't have seen otherwise. I may have lost my dear wife, but I have gained the peace of the Al-Anon program." Like yet another member, some of us are grateful just to be able to feel: "I am so deeply grateful for the grief I am experiencing. It sure beats the days when I was numb and stumbling through life."

While it's important to acknowledge our losses while we are grieving, gratitude can help us recognize what we do have. In the midst of life's impermanence, gratitude reminds us to appreciate each moment. As one member pointed out, "I can always find something to be grateful for, even if it's only my thumbs."

How do we practice gratitude? Some members have found it helpful to write a gratitude list on a regular basis. Others have developed a daily practice of saying thank you for small things, even for difficult moments and what they have to teach us. We learn to trust that we are exactly where we are supposed to be at this very moment. Pain and joy often coexist side by side. Gratitude is not about ignoring life's problems and difficulties. Rather, it's about recognizing that life isn't all or nothing.

"Al-Anon has opened my eyes, my ears, and my heart to the wonderful world I live in."

Gratitude can deepen our perspective and expand our sense of the world. It can help us appreciate our lives more fully. When we are less distracted and less focused on the alcoholic, we are more able to appreciate the small beauties of the world around us. Even in the midst of turmoil and grief, we can feel connected to our hearts. We might find that we are suddenly more aware of sunrises or sunsets, the songs of birds at dusk, a child's smile, or an animal's warm fur. Those things we once took for granted or didn't notice become the very things we rely on to nurture our spirits.

> *"I was powerless over the death of my husband, but I had choices about what to make of my life from that point on. I could choose to be bitter and angry that my husband was gone, or I could be grateful for the time we had together. I could choose to look at life as something to be endured alone, or I could embrace every precious moment. I could choose to look at my future with fear, or I could think of it as an adventure waiting to unfold."*

Each day is a chance for a new beginning. We can allow our grief to open our hearts to life's mysteries. Though we may not be able to control our losses, we learn that we still have choices in how we handle them. We may never be able to make sense of them, but we can find freedom in not having to understand everything.

> *"I'll probably never know why some people are able to find recovery while others are not. Still, I'm astonished to discover that not only in spite of, but because of my losses, I am more keenly aware of the tenuousness, the delicacy, and the beauty of every moment."*

Hope for today

> *"In Al-Anon I've learned that despite all my losses, there is still hope."*

So much of our recovery in Al-Anon is about striving to live in the present moment. When we can focus on today, we find that our fears about the future and worries about the past no longer dominate our lives as they once did. By learning how to manage this day only, we make a commitment to building a better life for ourselves. The reflections from our *Just for Today* bookmark have helped many of us as we strive to make the most of the present moment.

> *"Serenity doesn't come by avoiding the difficulties in my life, but by walking through them with the help of my Higher Power and my recovering friends."*

The goal of recovery is not to eliminate challenges entirely. Being human, we will all experience them from time to time. We can still find serenity even in the midst of our turmoil. Al-Anon can be a source of comfort and support as we face the unknown.

> *"Today I'm absolutely confident that whatever heartaches life brings, my beloved Al-Anon program will be there to hold my hand and gently walk with me."*

When we agree to take this journey into grief, we say yes to living life more fully. As we put our trust in Al-Anon and in our Higher Power, we are given the strength to face our losses—and for some of us, they are many. We learn that healing from our losses takes time, and we give ourselves permission to grieve for as long as we need. We keep coming back, even when we don't feel like it. We open our hearts, we share, and we listen—and little by little, we begin to heal.

Members share experience, strength, and hope: Spiritual growth from grieving

During the past year, I've had to accept some tough situations, including my son distancing himself from me. It's been over a year since I've seen my granddaughter. When my son first told me I was a bad parent and grandparent, I couldn't discuss the situation without crying. I've now come to realize that I can't change the situation or take away my son's problems. I now accept that he has to deal with his issues in his own way.

I've worked hard at turning the situation over to God as I try to move forward with my life. I continue to pray for my son's family and that God will take care of them. When my son is ready to let me back into his life, I plan to be ready to accept the offer with no bitterness or regrets. I've tried to remain positive in my correspondence with my son's family, even though communication is a one-way street right now.

Al-Anon has taught me so much and has given me the tools I need to face this current crisis in my life. I got up this morning and made the decision to make the coming year the best one ever. It's so true—life is what I make of it. I've learned that I'm worth a better life, and it's up to me to go out there and find it. Thank you, Al-Anon, for helping me see I have choices.

———————————————

Alcoholism has been called a robber and a thief because it steals so much from those of us affected by it. I have faced many losses as a result of growing up with this family disease. First and foremost, alcoholism robbed me of my capacity to feel my emotions. So when my parents divorced, I tried not to feel anything. When my father left, I blocked my grief. Each time another loss surfaced over the years, I succeeded in burying it.

Years later, I entered the rooms of Al-Anon and very slowly began to thaw out from this emotionally frozen condition. As time passed, divorce, geographic separation, and death brought losses to my life. With each loss, the Al-Anon tools and fellowship were there to support me, but only to the extent that I allowed. I still feared being consumed by my grief, and I felt safer stuffing my feelings than feeling them. I worried that if I started to cry, I wouldn't be able to stop. When my mother died, I barely cried and became depressed for months.

Finally, one particular loss brought me to a place where I could truly experience my grief. A close friend was diagnosed with a brain tumor. He was optimistic about treatment and anticipated a full and quick recovery. However, his surgery did not go as planned and he experienced severe complications. Though he was still alive, the person I knew and loved was gone. As I stepped into the role of caregiver for my friend, I felt as though I was on an emotional roller-coaster. It was much like dealing with an active alcoholic.

I constantly felt off balance. Every time I thought I knew what to expect, things changed. Al-Anon was there for me through the countless ups and downs. I increased my attendance at meetings and prayed with the fervor of a newcomer. I reminded myself daily of the "courage to change the things I can." I found myself doing things I had spent a lifetime convincing myself I was incapable of doing.

Through my dear friend's long medical ordeal and eventual death, I grew emotionally and spiritually in ways I never could have imagined. For the first time, I felt the intense pain of losing someone I love. I knew it was no longer an option to suffer in silence and solitude. I shared openly about my feelings and I wept. I have Al-Anon to thank for helping me see I had a choice to stop blocking my feelings and start experiencing them.

My experiences with loss have shown me how much I've grown in Al-Anon. I have lost three close family members. The contrast in how I felt at the time of each death tells me just how much I've changed.

My mother died two years before I found Al-Anon, while I was still coping with my wife's active alcoholism. I felt nothing when my mother died, and I couldn't understand why. My Mum and I had a good, loving relationship, so why couldn't I cry? Then my wife found sobriety, and I found Al-Anon.

When the time came for my dad to die, I had been in Al-Anon for eight years. After his death, I felt a physical pain in my heart that had not been there for my Mum. At the time, I had no idea what had happened to make me feel differently. My younger, alcoholic brother died just six years later. By that time, I had been in Al-Anon for 14 years. When my brother died, I experienced grief in an even deeper way.

I believe that Al-Anon has changed me from a man with no apparent feelings into a man who can feel. I do not use the word "normal," as I don't know what that means. Before Al-Anon, I wasn't really functioning emotionally. Now my feelings are very real. These three deaths were like milestones on the road to my recovery in Al-Anon, for which I am extremely grateful.

I had been in Al-Anon for eight years when I decided that taking care of myself meant leaving my marriage. I had a Sponsor and was working the Steps, but I found myself feeling more and more disconnected. All this time, I thought I had been in Al-Anon for me. Now that my marriage was over, I realized how much it had been about wanting my husband to find recovery. I was mourning for the death of my dreams. For a long time, I couldn't even say those words without crying.

My Sponsor and Al-Anon friends suggested I needed to grieve. They told me that grief was a process and that someday I would find myself on the other side of it. Back then, even going to meetings was an effort. I remember sitting there and hardly hearing anything that was being said. But I kept going, I started sharing, and I trusted that this program would bring me through my grief. And it did. There is another side to grief and it's wonderful. It's a feeling and experience I would never have known if I hadn't kept my commitment to the Al-Anon program. Today I have no regrets, but I have much gratitude.

Questions for reflection and meditation

• How have I grown in self-awareness since coming to Al-Anon?

• What is my concept of "recovery" and what do I expect from it?

• Have I considered the benefits of making a gratitude list at times when I feel more resentment than gratitude?

• Has my concept of a spiritual awakening changed since beginning in Al-Anon?

• What parts of my life have been awakened since my time in recovery?

• How have my losses helped shape the person I am becoming today?

Guide to Additional Readings on Grief and Loss

Though this book is devoted entirely to grief and loss, much of our literature in Al-Anon touches upon this subject. Additional readings on grief and loss can be found in the following literature:

- *...In All Our Affairs* (B-15)
- *Courage to Change* (B-16)
- *From Survival to Recovery* (B-21)
- *How Al-Anon Works* (B-22)
- *Courage to Be Me* (B-23)
- *Living Today in Alateen* (B-25)
- *Hope for Today* (B-27)
- *Living with Sobriety* (P-49)
- *The Forum* magazine

Twelve Steps

Study of these Steps is essential to progress in the Al-Anon program. The principles they embody are universal, applicable to everyone, whatever his personal creed. In Al-Anon, we strive for an ever-deeper understanding of these Steps, and pray for the wisdom to apply them to our lives.

1. We admitted we were powerless over alcohol—that our lives had become unmanageable.
2. Came to believe that a Power greater than ourselves could restore us to sanity.
3. Made a decision to turn our will and our lives over to the care of God *as we understood Him.*
4. Made a searching and fearless moral inventory of ourselves.
5. Admitted to God, to ourselves, and to another human being the exact nature of our wrongs.
6. Were entirely ready to have God remove all these defects of character.
7. Humbly asked Him to remove our shortcomings.
8. Made a list of all persons we had harmed, and became willing to make amends to them all.
9. Made direct amends to such people wherever possible, except when to do so would injure them or others.
10. Continued to take personal inventory and when we were wrong promptly admitted it.
11. Sought through prayer and meditation to improve our conscious contact with God *as we understood Him,* praying only for knowledge of His will for us and the power to carry that out.
12. Having had a spiritual awakening as the result of these steps, we tried to carry this message to others, and to practice these principles in all our affairs.

Twelve Traditions

These guidelines are the means of promoting harmony and growth in Al-Anon groups and in the worldwide fellowship of Al-Anon as a whole. Our group experience suggests that our unity depends upon our adherence to these Traditions:

1. Our common welfare should come first; personal progress for the greatest number depends upon unity.

2. For our group purpose there is but one authority—a loving God as He may express Himself in our group conscience. Our leaders are but trusted servants—they do not govern.

3. The relatives of alcoholics, when gathered together for mutual aid, may call themselves an Al-Anon Family Group, provided that, as a group, they have no other affiliation. The only requirement for membership is that there be a problem of alcoholism in a relative or friend.

4. Each group should be autonomous, except in matters affecting another group or Al-Anon or AA as a whole.

5. Each Al-Anon Family Group has but one purpose: to help families of alcoholics. We do this by practicing the Twelve Steps of AA *ourselves*, by encouraging and understanding our alcoholic relatives, and by welcoming and giving comfort to families of alcoholics.

6. Our Family Groups ought never endorse, finance or lend our name to any outside enterprise, lest problems of money, property and prestige divert us from our primary spiritual aim. Although a separate entity, we should always co-operate with Alcoholics Anonymous.

7. Every group ought to be fully self-supporting, declining outside contributions.

8. Al-Anon Twelfth Step work should remain forever non-professional, but our service centers may employ special workers.

9. Our groups, as such, ought never be organized; but we may create service boards or committees directly responsible to those they serve.

10. The Al-Anon Family Groups have no opinion on outside issues; hence our name ought never be drawn into public controversy.

11. Our public relations policy is based on attraction rather than promotion; we need always maintain personal anonymity at the level of press, radio, films, and TV. We need guard with special care the anonymity of all AA members.

12. Anonymity is the spiritual foundation of all our Traditions, ever reminding us to place principles above personalities.

Twelve Concepts of Service

The Twelve Steps and Traditions are guides for personal growth and group unity. The Twelve Concepts are guides for service. They show how Twelfth Step work can be done on a broad scale and how members of a World Service Office can relate to each other and to the groups, through a World Service Conference, to spread Al-Anon's message worldwide.

1. The ultimate responsibility and authority for Al-Anon world services belongs to the Al-Anon groups.
2. The Al-Anon Family Groups have delegated complete administrative and operational authority to their Conference and its service arms.
3. The right of decision makes effective leadership possible.
4. Participation is the key to harmony.
5. The rights of appeal and petition protect minorities and insure that they be heard.
6. The Conference acknowledges the primary administrative responsibility of the Trustees.
7. The Trustees have legal rights while the rights of the Conference are traditional.
8. The Board of Trustees delegates full authority for routine management of Al-Anon Headquarters to its executive committees.
9. Good personal leadership at all service levels is a necessity. In the field of world service the Board of Trustees assumes the primary leadership.
10. Service responsibility is balanced by carefully defined service authority and double-headed management is avoided.
11. The World Service Office is composed of selected committees, executives and staff members.
12. The spiritual foundation for Al-Anon's world services is contained in the General Warranties of the Conference, Article 12 of the Charter.

General Warranties of the Conference

In all proceedings the World Service Conference of Al-Anon shall observe the spirit of the Traditions:

1. that only sufficient operating funds, including an ample reserve, be its prudent financial principle;
2. that no Conference member shall be placed in unqualified authority over other members;
3. that all decisions be reached by discussion vote and whenever possible by unanimity;
4. that no Conference action ever be personally punitive or an incitement to public controversy;
5. that though the Conference serves Al-Anon it shall never perform any act of government; and that like the fellowship of Al-Anon Family Groups which it serves, it shall always remain democratic in thought and action.

Index